D1124878

This book is an autobiography and is based on true events. Names have been changed to protect the privacy of certain individuals.

Vickie Stringer Publishing
PO Box 247378
Columbus, Ohio 43224.
www.TripleCrownPublications.com

Library of Congress Control Number:
ISBN 13: 978-0-9820996-3-6

Publisher: Vickie M. Stringer
Cover design: Valerie Thompson, Leap Graphics
Photographer: Treagen Kier Colston
Makeup: George McKenney
Hair: Javon Pinellas
Stylist: Charles Wade

Printed in the United States of America

FIRST TRADE PAPERBACK EDITION PRINTING JUNE 2009

10 9 8 7 6 5 4 3 2

# Vixen Icon

## Buffie Carruth

# ACKNOWLEDGEMENTS

I would like to thank GOD! Life, happiness and success are not even possible without Him!

Thanks to Vickie Stringer & Triple Crown Publications for making my dream of being an author a reality!

You know my family comes first, which I love dearly! Mary Marable (GREATEST MOTHER IN THE ENTIRE WORLD!); my brothers and sisters, Ricky Marable, Judy Carruth, Jennifer Hardy, Charles Hardy Jr. and Andre Hardy; my nieces and nephews, Ashley Pittard, Ricky Marable Jr., Andre Hardy Jr., Jordan Hull, Jason Carruth, Rachel Marable, Brianna Pattmon, Micheal Pattmon Jr.; my brother-in-law Micheal Pattmon; Alfred Davis (my backbone…love you); my stepfather Charles Hardy, and my father, Willie Raidford.

Thanks to Perris Hull (we had a lot of good times!), Amina Diop (you were EVERYTHING that I needed in this industry...I can never give you enough thanks), Eric Parker (thanks for all your help and I mean ALL OF IT...priceless), Bernard Jamerson (Greensboro, NC), Rawle Stewart (thanks for being there for that support and not letting me give up), Reco Cross (my longtime homie), Ray Stewart (Atlanta, GA), Anthony Gist (Columbia, SC), Anthony Burgess (Philly, PA), Tommy Nelson (my Baltimore dogg!), Chuck Veney (Baltimore, MD), Blue Green (Athens, GA), Billy Willis (Houston, TX), Dwayne Darden (summerbunnies. com...we went through a lot together in the beginning), Sean Malcolm (KING Magazine...thanks for believing in me), Troy Hairston (security), Barry Murdock (datamatrixit. com), DJ Kayslay (thanks for making me see that "going backwards" is not an option), Leon Adams (my tailor... thanks for making all my jeans fit my waist), Danny Sanders, Sean Rush, Theralyn Lewis, G Flixx, VanSilk, Javon Pinellas (hairstylist), George McKenney (makeup artist...making me look so pretty!), Derrick Bray (dglobal. net), Big Bloc Entertainment, Ujaama Talent Agency, Inc., Christopher Nolen, my attorney Uwonda Carter, my trainers Antonio Williams, Jerome Biggers and Cory Robinson, Treagen Kier (photographer), Chip (Heiesuke.com), Quincy Hartsfield, Terrence Davidson, Azzure Denim (thanks for all the clothes), Ruff Ryders (YOU KNOW!!!), Scott (National Mail Services, Columbia, SC), BlackMen Magazine, Smooth Magazine, XXL Magazine and FEDS Magazine.

# INTRODUCTION

S tar. Legend. Icon. Videos, magazines, Web and radio features all played a role in cultivating this iconic superwoman that the world has embraced and marveled at since 2005. I am privileged to simply know her as Buffie Carruth, my friend. Very few people have had as profound an effect in my lifetime as Buffie has had. She is a constant inspiration not only to me, but to men and women around the world, to never let up.

When we initially met back in January 2005, I had no idea that she would become one of the most distinguished figures (pun intended) in urban model history. The superhighway to fame and fortune had begun; she's unmistakable.

In 2007, after she had hosted a party in Houston, Texas, we went to visit a local strip club that she used to work in.  The dancer on stage looked totally disinterested as she moved rhythmically around the pole.  I looked over at Buffie, and she was staring with a glazed-over look.  She then leaned over and said to me, "If I ever had to go back to doing this, I think I'd kill myself."  I knew she meant it.  I also know with 100 percent certainty that she would never have to do anything she doesn't want to do again.  Her will and drive are far too strong.

Buffie's influence in the urban model genre has been and will continue to be highly impacting for years to come.  She has redefined how the world views "models," making a strong statement about how breathtaking dark-skinned, thick women truly are.  Be encouraged.  As Buffie has proved, never say never.

Dwyane Darden
*SummerBunnies.com*

# Chapter One

Yes, my name really is Buffie, Buffie Carruth. My mother got my name from a TV show that used to air in the late sixties called *Family Affair*. I grew up in Athens, Georgia, in the seventies and eighties. Athens is probably only famous for the University of Georgia, REM, and I suppose by this time, myself. Athens is located in the northeastern part of the state and is Southern as hell. The county schools weren't desegregated until 1970, if that gives you an idea of how Southern it was.

My mother had seven kids. There were four girls and three boys, with me being the third oldest. My sisters are named Judy, Jennifer, and Atline, and my brothers are named Ricky, Charles, and Andre in that order. You can place me right in between Judy and Jennifer.

You would probably assume that we didn't have

much because of seven siblings, and your guess is right. I can say that although we were less fortunate than most, we always had the necessities, like a home, food, and clothes. Like most American children and teenagers, I felt that having the bare necessities weren't good enough, and these feelings had a great influence on the paths I've taken in life.

My mother was never married to my father. She did marry Charles, the father of my younger siblings. He left and moved to Chicago, where he was originally from, when I was in the eighth grade, and I've been fatherless ever since. Growing up, my mother never allowed me to associate with my biological father. In her eyes, I only had one father, and that's the man she was married to.

My real father tried to be in my life, but my mother was a little selfish. All she wanted from him was those child support checks to keep rolling in, and I don't blame her because times were hard, but any kind of contact was out. It wasn't fair to me, but what could I do? I had three stepsisters on my father's side, but I couldn't associate with them either. Until I was just about grown, I never really had much contact with my father. After I became an adult, I felt as if it was too late to try to build a relationship with him. Today, my father and I are on good terms, and we speak from time to time, and I know it wasn't his fault that he wasn't in my life.

I lived in two low-income housing projects when I was very young. Nellie B. was on the east side of town, and after living there for a time, we stayed at Bethel Church Homes, which was located in downtown Athens. Neither of them were bad places back then, and I liked both spots. I preferred Nellie B., because the buildings were much larger and more spread out. I had more room to play.

I really don't remember many details about living in the projects because I was so young, but I do remember being happy, having a lot of toys, and having my first birthday party. I don't remember the projects being dirty or violent. From what I do remember, they were regular apartments for people with low incomes. I don't remember my older siblings, Judy and Ricky, fighting with the other kids. I don't remember my mother and father having any beef with the neighbors. I just remember me and my brother Charles, who is a year younger than I, riding on our Big Wheels and having no worries. I don't remember any bad times in the projects, not at all. Seems like the projects was the place to be in those days, as hard as it may be to believe considering how they are now.

After the projects, we moved around a lot, bouncing from a house, to a mobile home, from my grandmother's to Chicago for a time, and then again from my grandmother's to a home I would live in until I became an adult. I lived in different places as a kid but always with the same people: my mother, my stepfather, and my sisters and brothers. No matter what, we were always together.

My mother never really worked. She was at home with

us 24/7. My mom had seven kids, so it was almost impossible to work and pay for daycare. My stepfather always worked, and my mother stayed home and raised us. My mother was incredibly protective of her children. I don't ever remember her leaving us at anyone's house while she ran the streets. If it wasn't my grandmother babysitting us, then it was no one. I'm sure a lot of moms work now and raise kids at the same time, but many things have changed since the seventies.

My mother is extremely proud of how far I've come. She still lives in Athens, so people constantly ask her how I'm doing. She calls me every day, telling me that some girl or guy said hello. There would always be a female or guy claiming that we were best friends or they used to date me. Most of the time I don't even know who they are, and it doesn't help that my mother always forgets their name.

Oh, and don't let someone say something negative to my mother about what I do for a living. She will jump all down their throat. I tell her all the time to slow her roll. You can't be tripping on people just because someone has an opinion or wants to be a hater. She knows I don't deal with many people from my hometown because of some of the comments I've heard in the past. I'm social when I go back to my hometown, but I don't hang out much.

We didn't have much in life, but I can say we had each other, and my mother definitely loved us without a doubt, and everyone knew this. We were not allowed to sleep over at other people's houses, and no one could sleep over ar our house. We were not allowed to eat at other people's houses either, and if she thought for a split second that we were in trouble or someone was bothering one of her kids, she was there, even if she had to walk!

We were on welfare all of our childhood and teenage years. I never had new clothes unless it was the first day of school. Our clothes were always secondhand from yard sales and Goodwill stores. In elementary school, I never wore the pretty, ruffled dresses and bright, candy-colored bows or ribbons in my hair like most of the little girls. I remember a few times stealing other girls' bows from their hair when the teacher would sit us on the floor for story time. I would prey on the girl with the prettiest bows, and I would sit directly behind her and steal half the ribbons from her hair. I would wait a few days and then wear them back to school in my hair. I even pushed my best friend down during recess on picture day one time just to get her dress dirty so my dress could look better than hers. Her dress *still* looked prettier.

Believe it or not, I was always skinny most of my life. I really didn't have any fat people in my immediate family. Hell, yes, I hated being skinny! I felt that being skinny wasn't attractive at all. I didn't have a problem finding clothes, but who cares? That was the least of my worries. Growing up in the South back in the seventies, I often heard older people say, "You look unhealthy if you're too skinny." I remember my grandmother telling me to get in the kitchen and put some meat on my bones!

Eating healthy to them was chicken fried in lard, cornbread from scratch (no Jiffy), black-eyed peas, cabbage, neck bones, rice and gravy, collard greens seasoned with ham hocks and fatback, and some sweet tea or Kool-Aid. Damn, that was some good eating back then! Now you try and mention something about those old cooking methods and bloggers and health nuts will chew your ass up. You almost have to sneak and eat that food now. I hate when these "modernized" people try to tell me what's not good for me. I say, fuck 'em!

Most black guys, young and old, northern or southern, haven't ever found being skinny to be sexy, and I knew this as a teenager. I noticed how guys were so crazy about my older sister Judy when I was growing up. She had all the good guys! They all had cars, they were cute, and they used to always bring her gifts and take her out. She had a nice shape. She had a big butt and hips to match, but no stomach at all. She had thick, jet-black hair that she used to set on big, pink sponge rollers every night for school the next morning. She even has a beauty mole right above her lip. I wanted to be just like her. She wasn't skinny, so why was I?

I often got depressed because I wasn't thick. All my life through school I've noticed that girls had to be cute and pretty, or you had to be fine as hell with some ass and hips to be an "in" girl. Even if you didn't have big breasts, it was cool as long as you had some ass. I didn't have any breasts, no ass, and no hips, and that shit made me feel so insecure. I looked like a little damn boy! I felt like I was an average-looking female but nothing to write home to mom about. All through school, my self-esteem was never really on point.

I had a few boyfriends through school, but none of them were football players, owned a car, or were even popular. Those types of guys were reserved for the popular girls. I remember a few of my friends who had nice, shapely bodies. I was so jealous of them because they seemed to have it all — and they did, from the outside looking in. They had the cute guys lusting over them, they wore the flyest clothes, and all the girls wanted to be their friends (including me). They were the "shot callers" of the clique that hung with them. I hated school. I just wish I had then what I have now. I would have been untouchable.

# Chapter Two

My shoplifting game was on point. There was nothing I couldn't get. It started when I was in the seventh grade. I was just sick and tired of never having anything nice. I was also hanging with the wrong crowd, let my mother tell it. By age 14, I was stealing every day. I shoplifted from the seventh grade until I was out of high school. My mother couldn't stop me, and I wasn't going to stop on my own, that's for sure. I was never into selling the things I stole. I needed the clothes; selling was not an option.

Everyone in my family had what they wanted. My little brother had every transformer toy that they made. After school every day, my friends and I would go across the street to a store called Big G and we would steal our asses off. I never dressed well in school until I started stealing. My wardrobe got a lot better, so my self-esteem went up a little, but when it came to the popular girls, I still couldn't even compare. I still didn't have the body. Regardless, I chose to continue my rampages, because having something was better than having nothing.

I would carry a big purse, making sure it wasn't large enough to raise suspicion. Sometimes I would stuff items down the front or the back of the waist of my pants. I would always lift during the day when there weren't many customers browsing the stores.

If it was a piece of clothing I was trying to steal, I would take it off the hanger and hide the hanger either between the clothes or on the floor under the clothing racks. I would wrap the garment tight and stuff it in my purse or under my shirt. If it wasn't in a box or package, I would unwrap it and hide the empty packaging behind another box or on the back shelf out of sight. I would never leave a hanger or empty package in plain sight for someone to walk by and instantly see.

My shoplifting friends would come to school dressed alike, and people started rumors that we were shoplifting. I didn't give a damn—I had new clothes, and that's all that mattered. It didn't make me more popular, but at least I wasn't getting teased because my clothes weren't nice.

The summer right before I entered high school, I was caught shoplifting at Richway, a department store. By this time, I had already been to court more than once for shoplifting, and the judge wasn't trying to hear that shit this go-around! He'd had enough of me. He committed me to the state of Georgia for 3 years.

Right there in the courtroom, he made me remove my jewelry and empty my pockets. I turned to give my mother my belongings, but she had already left the courtroom in tears. My oldest sister had taken her place on the bench directly behind me. I handed my sister my jewelry and pocket contents and walked out of the courtroom in handcuffs.

Once I was outside, I noticed my sister and mother standing in front of the Federal Building. It was clear that my mother wasn't holding it together at all. My sister was crying too but not as badly as my mother. I stepped into the transportation van and didn't look back. I couldn't hold back my tears once I was inside the van. I couldn't believe what just happened to me in that courtroom. I really lost it then. I was crying like my mother had just died.

I was taken to Gainesville, Georgia, an hour from Athens. I was detained in a juvenile facility for about 4 weeks. My mother came to visit me every weekend for the 4 weeks I was there. After staying that month in the facility, I was taken to my mother's house to pack my clothes and the state sent me to live in a contract home in Statham, Georgia, with another family. It was very similar to being in foster care.

I would live with that family for a little over 2 years. There I had to complete a 6-week program called Project Challenge. If I happened to get kicked out of the program before it was completed, I would go back to a lockup facility for the remainder of my 3 years. In the program, we had to learn to follow directions as a group and to work together. We camped out in the woods in tents. We hiked, completed team-building activities, sat in groups talking about our problems, had lots of exercise and prepared dinner for the whole group. The program didn't help me at all, and I can't say if it helped any of the kids that I was there with.

I finished the program, but I was still shoplifting with one of the other girls who lived in the contract home with me. I feel like the only way I would have stopped stealing earlier was to be sent off to prison. I kept shoplifting because I liked nice things, and I couldn't afford to buy them. It was that simple. I didn't think I was a bad person and didn't understand the connection between the program and my need for clothes and hygiene products. I did, eventually, start stealing even if I had a little money in my pockets, but I never did have enough to cover all of my daily living needs.

The girl I stole with during my time in the contract home was actually the daughter of the lady who ran the juvenile program. On the weekends, I would go stealing with her and her cousins. All of her cousins were shoplifters, and they all became my best friends after I left the contract home and moved back home with my mother.

While living with my new family in Statham, I experienced sex for the first time with a boy who lived around the corner, Derek. He was so fine! He had good hair, and he had a smooth, baby-brown complexion. Even though he was thin, he was bow-legged and very tempting to me.

I remember Derek calling me one evening and asking me to come up to his house. It was just about dark so I knew I had to hurry back. I walked to his house, which was four houses away from mine. He was standing outside when I walked up to his yard.

"What's up?" he asked.

"You," I replied.

"Want to go walkin'?"

"Sure," I shrugged my shoulders and smiled. The whole time I was sure I was going to get in trouble because it was dark now.

I followed Derek three houses down to a neighbor's home, and we walked across the yard. I continued to follow him around the back of the house, wondering where in the hell we were going. Finally, we came to a picnic table in the backyard. He stepped up on the table and sat down.

"Come here," he commanded. I walked closer to him and stood between his legs, resting my elbows on his knees. He started kissing me and rubbing my chest. I couldn't believe I was kissing him with his fine ass!

Derek kept kissing me, and he slowly moved his hands lower. He started unbuttoning my jeans. I pushed his hands away as we continued kissing. He pulled me even closer and tried to unbutton my jeans again. This time I didn't stop him. I was nervous as hell. What if someone was out walking and happened to see us?

After we got my jeans unzipped, he told me to pull them off.

"Lie down," he said. I did what I was told. As I lay there watching him remove his pants, I got so nervous that my knees started shaking. I just closed my eyes. *Fuck it, you only live once!*

Derek stepped up on the table and lay down between my legs. Before I could realize that he was in, it was over. He quickly got up and put his jeans back on. I sat up on the table, fumbling for my jeans and trying not to make eye contact with him because I was a little embarrassed for him. After I got dressed, we walked back to the street without exchanging words.

"I'll call you later," he said when we got to his house.

"Okay, cool," I said quickly and sped off to my house.

The whole walk home, I was wondering what he was thinking. The silence we had on the way back to the house was so puzzling. I tried to just get it off my mind. I had tried sex before with another guy from my hometown when I was living with my mother, but it hurt so badly that I never went through with it and made him stop. But tonight, I never felt it going in. I knew it was in—and out—very quickly. So is this how sex really is? Is it really this boring and quick? Oh well, at least I got my first time out of the way. I was halfway to being a woman, and I could finally join in conversations with my friends when they talked about having sex. Every girl that was ever my friend growing up had already had sex before me. I was always the last one to do anything when it came to boys. I wouldn't even give any "favors" to a guy until almost 10 years later.

The family I was living with while I was committed to the state moved to Commerce, Georgia. In Commerce, I met Lamont, my very first real boyfriend. I went on to date him for over 7 years. By the time the judge and my social worker decided to let me move back home with my mother after almost 3 years, I was pregnant.

I've always considered Lamont my first true love, because he was my first real relationship. We were about the same age. He was a shy, slim-built type of guy that had cute eyes. He was a regular dude from a pretty nice family. He lived with his mother, but his father didn't live far away. I fell in love with him, and I loved him to death. After school every day, he worked part time at the local hospital in his hometown, and my after-school job, when I moved back home, was at this steakhouse that was located inside the mall. I knew Lamont was looking forward to this child, and

I know he would have been a great father.

Lamont was still living in Commerce, and I was back in Athens with my mother. I had dropped out of school when I came back to live with my mother because I didn't want to be at school pregnant amongst people who may have given me grief over it. My mother found a school for expecting mothers to attend, so after only a few weeks, I went back to school and graduated.

One evening, I was dancing in the living room of my mother's house, trying to imitate MC Hammer on TV (my idol at the time). I started bleeding later that night. I called my older sister Judy and told her what was going on. She came and picked me up and took me to the emergency room, where they kept me overnight. The doctor informed me that I was having a miscarriage. They had to scrape my womb, which was excruciating and very uncomfortable.

I stayed at the hospital that night by myself. My mother called to see if I was okay, and I told her I was, so there was no need for her to come to the hospital. I cried all night because I was so looking forward to having my baby. After the miscarriage, I never had the desire to have children.

When I finally graduated from high school, I got caught shoplifting for the last time. I was 18. The judge, who operated outside of the juvenile system now that I was technically an adult, told me if I came to court one more time for shoplifting that he would send me to prison. I never shoplifted again. I just couldn't see myself being locked up for a long period of time and losing my freedom. By this time, one of my brothers had been in and out of prison for burglary, auto theft, and robbery. He had made a long career out of it, but I decided to give it up.

# Chapter Three

I'm sure everyone reaches a point where they have trouble caring about going on in life. I never thought I would be trying to kill myself over something my mother did.

I was just out of high school. I was fighting with Atline. I don't recall what the conflict was about, but I know it wasn't just a disagreement or an argument. We were literally fighting. Atline was spoiled as hell, so you couldn't even breathe on her or look at her too hard without getting scolded or kicked out of the house. Any time I got into it with her, it was always for her own good or trying to stop her from disrespecting my mother or one of the other siblings. And I was always the one who would get in trouble for trying to make her act right.

Whatever I was fighting with her about, it got out of

of hand and I lashed out and hit her with a closed fist. She started crying and went bananas, swinging and acting crazy, trying to charge me. So we started fighting in the living room of my mother's house where we were both living at the time. My mother came out of the bedroom and grabbed me and cursed me and told me to get the fuck out of her house. Didn't ask no questions and she didn't want to hear no explanations.

Everybody seemed mad at me; no one was trying to help me explain what had happened. No one would listen—not even my other siblings who were there at the time. It was nighttime and winter. It was cold as hell outside, but I went to my room, grabbed my shit, and ran out the door, slamming it so hard that the picture hanging by the door fell and broke. I was so mad and upset I started crying. I didn't have anywhere to go, and I didn't have a car. I was so disgusted with my family that I felt like dying. I felt like everyone was against me, and no one cared. If you don't have family, who do you have?

I should have known my brother and sister weren't going to jump on my side, because they didn't want to be kicked out on the streets just like me. I walked up the street to my friend Jay's house. He liked me, but I would never give him any real play. He was a nice guy, but I just wasn't attracted to him. I thought he was too old, and he smoked like a train. I've never been attracted to guys who smoked cigarettes, because it smelled horrible and it doesn't make a person cute or sexy to have a nasty ass cigarette stuck out of the side of their mouth. Growing up, I remembered the only people who smoked were old people and alcoholics, and they certainly weren't appealing to the eye.

I think Jay was in his thirties. I did kiss him a few times, and just as I imagined, his breath smelled like an ashtray. He would give me rides, so I had to be friendly.

I knocked on his door, and he answered. "Jay, I feel horrible, and I need somewhere to go tonight." I didn't want to go inside his house because he lived with family. "Can we just go and stay at a hotel tonight?" I asked.

"Yea, sure," he said as he turned to go back inside to get dressed. I stood at his front door while he went back inside and got himself together. He came out, and we left. As we drove, I told him about what happened and threatened out loud that I would fix my family. I was never going back! I was so disgusted with my mother I couldn't even explain. All I wanted to do was get her back and make her suffer the way I was.

We stopped at my mother's house on the way out of the neighborhood so I could grab some clothes. I knocked on the door, and she opened it, standing there looking at me like, "What?"

I brushed past her and mumbled, "I got to get something out my room." I went to my room, grabbed a few pieces of clothing, and went to the bathroom to get some personal hygiene products. I headed back to the front of the house where my mother was still standing with the door wide open. I walked out and got in the car with Jay and left. I saw her looking out, trying to figure out who I was riding with. I don't know if she recognized Jay's car or not. The way I was feeling, I didn't want her to know who I was with or where I was going. I wanted her to worry.

When I jumped back in the car with Jay, I started crying again. All I wanted to do was get my mother back for kicking me out of the house. The plan was already in my head before I went back to her house to get my clothes. I took a pill bottle out of my jacket pocket as I rode with Jay to the hotel. He wasn't paying me much attention because he was into the music and getting to the hotel, thinking that he was finally going to get a piece of ass from me, but little did he know ... I had grabbed a bottle of prescription pills from the medicine cabinet when I was in the bathroom at my mother's house and took them with me. I felt if I killed myself, then she would have to suffer and I wouldn't have to anymore.

I threw about 10 pills down my throat and swallowed without any water or liquid. Jay saw my head go back and my hand come down from my mouth out of the corner of his eye. He turned and looked at me.

"What the fuck did you just do?" He grabbed my right arm and saw the half-empty pill bottle open in my hand and went crazy!

"Are you fucking crazy? What the fuck's wrong with you?" He tried to snatch the bottle out of my hand. I quickly poured the rest of the pills in my hand, tossed the empty bottle into his lap and gulped the rest of the pills down my dry throat. He stopped the car in front of the hotel and started fussing with me.

"Buffie, talk to me!" he said. I just sat there, staring out of the window. He stood outside the car for almost 20 minutes trying to talk to me, but I wouldn't say a word. He finally stomped off into the hotel lobby and came back out and got into the car. I could tell he was mad, but he didn't say anything else. We went into the room, and he flopped on the bed and fell back and put his hands over his eyes. I turned the TV on and sat down in the chair by the window. He didn't say anything, and I didn't say anything. I just watched TV.

After about half an hour, I jumped up and ran to the bathroom. My stomach was cramping, and I was completely overcome with immense pain. I started throwing up everywhere—on the floor, bathtub, sink, everywhere except the toilet. I couldn't stand still because my stomach was so upset. I thought I was going to die.

Jay came in, and I could tell he was scared and worried as hell. He started frantically trying to pick me up off the floor, but there was so much vomit everywhere that he couldn't keep his grip on me without slipping on the floor.

"Let's go to the hospital now, Buffie!" he kept yelling, but I was too sick to move. I kept yelling in a sick voice, "No!"

He was begging me. "Please, Buffie, let me take you to the hospital!" After awhile, I let him help me up off the floor, and he walked me to his car and sped off to the emergency room. I don't ever remember being so sick in my life. I couldn't even see straight, so I had to keep my eyes closed because they weren't focusing at all. I felt halfway blind. I was so out of it I felt like opening the car door trying to jump out on the way to the hospital. Anything had to feel better than what I was going through right then!

We arrived at the hospital, and someone came out with a wheelchair. I could barely sit up straight in the chair. They wheeled me into this cold room with bright lights and helped me onto a bed, and that was it. I don't remember anything else.

When I woke up, Jay was sitting in the chair beside the bed, staring at me with my jacket in his hands. I could tell he was relieved but still a little upset because he just looked at me and didn't say anything. The doctor came in and explained to me what had happened. I just lay there crying, thinking what I had almost done to myself and my family. I was more ashamed of myself than anything. I was still feeling under the weather and weak, but nothing like I was a few hours before. I felt so empty inside, and all I wanted to do was go home to my family.

The doctor discharged me and made me an appointment to seek mental health counseling in the next few days. I didn't feel I needed counseling; I knew I had made a mistake and made an overemotional teenage decision. I just wanted to go home. The nurse rolled me out to Jay's car, which was waiting for me at the side door, and we left. He took me to my mother's house and said he would call me later to check on me. I walked up the driveway and knocked on my mother's door. She opened the door with her coffee and housecoat on. I walked in, and she closed the door behind me. I walked to my room and closed my door behind me. If she only knew what I had just went through.

As I write this chapter, I've mentioned this incident to a few people and told them that I was writing about it in my book. I couldn't believe how many women I know who had gone though similar situations. I'm sure there's a lot of "industry" people who go through this also. There's a lot of stress in this industry because you try so hard to stay relevant and make money at the same time. Now, I can't even imagine trying to commit suicide because someone pissed me off or for any other reason. I haven't had suicidal thoughts since that one time I tried it. I don't want to hurt my family.

My mother is a wonderful person, and I love her to death. The only people in the world that I have are my mother, my siblings, and my nieces and nephews. Sure, I've had aunts, uncles, grandmothers, and cousins, but I was never close to them growing up. I was close to my grandmother Carrie. She was my mother's mother. She died when I got out of high school, so that was it besides my immediate family.

My aunts were always traveling and lived in other cities, and I never kept in touch with uncles or cousins. I wasn't a mean child growing up, I was just strong-minded and always wanted to explore and step outside the box a little.

I wasn't the easiest child to raise because I was always somewhere trying to be different and experimental. My mother never condoned my terminated pregnancies. When I dropped out of school, she convinced me to go back. Any time I got in trouble, she was always there. When I was hurting for any reason, she would hurt. She's still my heart and my best friend, because I can talk to her about anything that goes on with me and she never judges me. I can talk to her about my career, hating females, relationships, and things that use to go on in the strip clubs when I was a dancer. She has met most of the guys I've dated; even if it wasn't a serious relationship, I still would bring them by to meet my mother. I can even talk to my mother about sex and give her all the dirty little details, and she would still listen and give me her opinion, even if in the back of her head she was thinking that her daughter was a freak. I know she only wants the best for her kids and having the best for her kids makes her happy. That's why anything I can do for her, I will, any chance I get.

I'd like to say that I was a good child after I stopped shoplifting and realized my suicide attempt wasn't worth the pain my mother would suffer if I hadn't made it. I hadn't quite caught on to the idea that life didn't have to be so rough. That being said, the rest of my young adulthood was filled with the kind of drama that would make any mother rip her hair out.

# Chapter Four

During the next couple of years, I earned my street cred. My mind-set wasn't focused on my future. After the shoplifting came the fighting. I was running the streets and didn't ever think about my future. There were a few girls that every time I saw them on the street, we just started fighting. I was up to my eyeballs in conflict. I also experienced a few unwanted pregnancies, three simple battery charges, one aggravated assault charge, one disorderly conduct charge, and almost a drug and counterfeit money charge.

Through this period in my life, Lamont stayed true to me and he didn't leave me, even though at that time, I was fighting, going to jail, and cheating. I realized eventually that I was on a dead-end path, but until then, I ran the streets with my girls and never thought twice about my actions.

The aggravated assault was a false charge. Out of the group of women my girls and I were fighting that particular night, one of them was stabbed in the chest. I knew who did it, but I wouldn't tell the police. Because I knew and didn't want to tell, I ended up getting charged with it. I tried to get the girl to fess up so I could be cleared of the charges, but she wouldn't confess. When I went to meet with the attorney and prosecutor, I finally told them the girl's name. They cleared and released me. I couldn't believe that stupid bitch was going to let me go to jail for some shit I didn't do! I never spoke to her again.

I used to ride with a metal baseball bat in the trunk of my car and a knife and gun under my seat. I never had the guts to stab anyone, but that wouldn't stop these other women from stabbing me. I even sprayed this one woman's mother with some mace because she was trying to defend her daughter and talking shit to me, so I sprayed the hell out of her. Her daughter ran out of the house and stabbed me in my leg.

I didn't even know I had been stabbed until the police came and I ran in one of the apartments in the projects where we had been fighting. I noticed my black jeans were wet, but I thought it was from falling in some water while I was fighting. Hell, no, it was blood, and my leg had started getting stiff, so my home girls convinced me to go to the hospital. I didn't want to go because I knew the police would come there and question me, but I went anyway. Just as I thought, the cops came. I told them I didn't know who had stabbed me. I lied because I didn't want them to lock this bitch up. I was planning on meeting her again on the street and fucking her up. I was rough in those days.

I used my baseball bat once. A girl had stabbed my lower arm in a fight. Those next few moments, I wasn't myself. I ran to my car, popped the trunk, and she was out cold when I stopped swinging. I was terrified that I had beaten her to death in my rage. I prayed to God that night like never before.

The next day, I found out that she was hospitalized. I was scared that the police would come to my mother's house and arrest me, but they never did. I decided that I wasn't taking any more chances and stopped carrying my bat around. I was a fighter, not a killer. I wasn't a punk when it came to fighting, but I was definitely a punk when it came to going to jail. I'd probably commit suicide if I got sentenced to prison.

My simple battery charge came from slapping a woman. She and I worked at the same grocery store, but I knew I couldn't get her at work. When I finished my shift one day, I went home, changed clothes, and came back to the store, sitting in my car across from the store in a parking lot. I watched her come out of the store and get in her car. I followed her for about a mile. The red light caught her on Baxter Street. I pulled up behind her, jumped out of the car, and walked up to the window of her car, reached my hand in her window and slapped the dog shit out of her, then I told her to get out. She didn't dare step out of the car. The light turned green, and she sped off. I jumped back in and followed her. She screamed at me out of the window that she was headed to the police station to press charges. That's when I turned off to another street.

Three weeks later, I got a letter in the mail from the Clarke County Magistrate. I already knew what it was before I opened it. Damn! Why couldn't she just hit me back? Why do these bitches want to see me got to jail? These females had so much mouth, but as soon as I put these little hands on them, they're ready to scream, "I'm pressing charges!" Back in the day, I would rather a female kick my ass then press charges on me. I believe in the saying, "If it starts in the streets, then let's keep it in the streets." Let's not get white people involved.

A few years after my miscarriage, Lamont became a well established drug dealer with fat pockets, a nice car, and bitches trying to get at him. His attitude never changed; he still was quiet and still living in Commerce with his mother. He bought me a car and was in Athens frequently. My mother would let him stay at her house because he was like part of the family. He would buy groceries for the family and give my little brother shoes. He was getting my hair done every week and he would take me shopping every weekend in Atlanta even though I had a job.

Lamont and I were always fighting and fussing. One night, our argument spilled out onto the street from a hotel room we had checked into. He slapped me so hard that I hit the street in front of the hotel. It was raining like hell that night, too. The hotel clerk saw the incident and called the police. The cops came and locked him up for disorderly conduct. They took him to jail, and I went home, got dressed, and went to the club that night. He got out the next morning, and my sister picked him up and brought him over to my mother's house where I was waiting. He apologized, and we were on again.

We eventually split up because I didn't come home one night when he spent the night at my mother's house. I didn't know that he was there. The next morning when I got there, he was getting ready to leave and go back to Commerce. I begged him to stay, put he just pushed me to the side and got in his car and left.

I've been very lucky. Out of all the trouble I'd been in since high school, I was never convicted of anything but misdemeanor shoplifting. After being stabbed four times in three different fights, one time in my hip and the other three times in my back and arm (one of the injuries left me so I couldn't walk for weeks), getting permanently scarred and bruised, going in and out of jail, almost being shot, and getting my hair snatched out and rocking a bald spot until my hair grew back—I realized if I didn't straighten up, I would end up killing someone or someone one would end up killing me. After 2 or 3 years of constant fighting, I gave it up. I learned to not worry about what people say to me or about me. I had too many war wounds on my body now to continue to act like a gangster. It just wasn't worth it anymore. My fighting phase was over in 1997.

# Chapter Five

How do I cut it? Where's the best place to sell it? How do you know who to sell it to? Who do you trust? What are the best hours of operation? Where do you keep your stash? And most niggas ain't trying to help you when they're hustling in the same game as you are.

My fighting days were gone, but I had one last hustle left in me. A friend of mine had gone to prison and left me some product. He really didn't want me selling it, but after I found out he wasn't getting out of prison anytime soon, I decided to take a chance. I couldn't talk to him on the phone while he was in prison about selling his dope, so I turned to someone else who knew a lot about drugs.

One of my best friends, Keke, was always down to

get dirty with me. She was a big help and familiar with the streets and the dope game. She was a fiend herself. We had been friends for over 6 years. She wasn't a friend that I could hang with to go and scout out sexy men, she wasn't a friend that I could go on vacations with, and she wasn't the friend that I could go clubbing with on the weekends. We were close as hell but in a different way. She knew all my family, and I knew hers. She hung out at my mom's house, and I would hang out at her folks' house. We would hang together all day, every day, just cruising in my '77 Buick Electra with the McLean wire spoke wheels and the 2-inch whitewalls.

I would never have to drive because she loved pushing the Buick with the fresh paint job, and she would even keep it clean for me. She smoked dope, and she drank 40s, but she was an excellent driver! I never knew whether she had a driver's license or not, but it didn't matter. All I know is Keke was my dog, and she was down for whatever!

She was a few years older than I, but I was more mature. She had kids, maybe four or five, but she didn't have custody of any of them. We would run into one of her children from time to time. She would always seem glad to see them, but she really couldn't do anything for them because she didn't have anything herself. She never had a car, and she never had a stable home. Every evening, I would drop her off at a different location. It was her sister's house, her grandmother's house, her cousin's house, or somewhere in the hood.

As long as she was with me she was always good. I worked at the grocery store around this time so I would hook up with her after work every day and we would hang until the sun went down. She would always disappear at night. She wouldn't call, and I wouldn't ever see her until the next morning, bright and early.

She was a booster, and anything I needed she would be sure to get. Since I had given up shoplifting and fighting, she had sort of stepped in and picked up where I left off. Boosting was her means of survival, and it supported her habit. Sometimes, I gave her my last dollar in exchange for some shit that I had seen at the mall. She never charged me for everything. She did look out for me and give me boosted items on the strength because at the end of the day, we were still friends and I was her main means of transportation. I would look out for her and buy her something to eat or provide transportation if she needed to get somewhere to make some money.

She's probably one of the closest friends I've had in my life. I used to miss her when she would go to jail for long periods of time. She would get convicted of shoplifting or probation violation at least once a year. I would send her money and accept her phone calls and sometimes even go and see her if she wasn't too far away. She had a fucked-up drug habit, but that didn't make her a bad person. My family loved her, and she was always my dog. I don't know how long she had been on drugs, but I wouldn't hesitate to say she's been an addict most of her life.

She was very protective of me. She didn't like anyone to say anything fucked up about me. She would always defend my character whenever she could. We would sometimes get up in the morning and go on a shoplifting spree all day until nightfall. I would go in the stores with her sometimes and pick out the things I wanted. Then I would leave the store and go and sit in the car and wait for her to come out. At the end of the day, my car would be loaded with hot merchandise from various stores. We would then make her rounds to her customers who had requested items, she would collect her money, I would drop her off at her place of choice, and we would meet again the next morning when she was broke and ready to make another run.

I cared enough about her where I wanted to tell her stop doing this, but I know the effect that cocaine has on people, and if she didn't do it with me, she would still continue to do it with someone else. After seeing her go to jail a few times, I no longer tried to stop her and just went with the flow. Her mind was always on getting that next hit or that next high. I know if I couldn't provide her with ways to make money to get that next high then I probably would never see her.

I understood her, and she understood me, and that's why we were so close. I never judged her, and I treated her like I would any other friend. Everyone in Athens knew that Keke was a junkie, but that was how she chose to live. She knew that I would never take her to buy dope and let her get back in the car with me. If she wanted to go and buy dope, I would take her and leave her there. No dope in my presence, and no dope in my car. When she wanted me to take her to someone, I always knew what she was going to do. We would never talk about it to each other, but she knew that I knew why she wanted to go where she wanted to go. It was like she was ashamed of me knowing that she smoked dope.

I never witnessed her in the actual act and never wanted to. I was curious on how to do it, but I didn't want to see someone I cared about do it in front of me. A guy friend of mine even offered Keke a free hit just so she could show me how it's done on a soda can. I could tell she was hesitant but willing to do it. I stopped her. I didn't think I could handle seeing her get high right in front of me.

When I went to Keke and told her I had dope that I wanted to sell, she was all for it. I called Keke one Sunday morning because I knew she'd be home.

"Hello?" Keke finally answered on the fourth ring.

"Get up, bitch. I know you ain't still asleep. Whatcha doing?"

"Shit, girl, just getting out of the bed. 'Bout to get in the shower," Keke muttered. It was obvious she'd had a rough night, and might even be high still.

"Well, shit, I wanna holla at you about something. Catch a ride over here when you get dressed," I said.

"Alright, Keith said he was going to pass by here, so I'll

have him drop me off over there." Keke hung up.

I was dressed and ready to ride when Keke got to the house. My mom let her in, and I quickly ushered her back to my room to tell her the plan.

"Shit, you ain't said nothing, bitch! Let's do it," Keke said. "You know I'm trying to get this money, Buffie."

I knew Keke would be all for this plan given her habit, but I still couldn't help but feel a little guilty about flaunting her bad habit in front of her like a carrot, but a bitch got to get paid, right?

"You know you came to the right one with this hustle, girl," Keke said as we were on our way to get our supplies. "This is going to be real easy. All we have to do is cut it down, bag it up, and hit the streets."

She and I bought razor blades from the supermarket and rented a hotel room to cut the drugs. Every guy I had dated back then was a drug dealer, so I knew what size to cut it, but she still showed me step by step. I wasn't selling weight, because I didn't have enough, so we had to do the street corner thing and sell 10s and 20s.

After we got it cut up and wrapped in plastic, Keke told me it would be best to wait until Friday, which happened to be the first of the month, and I could probably get rid of it all in one day. I thought that was easy enough, so I stashed the shit and waited until Friday.

Friday came, and I called Keke early that afternoon so she could meet me in Parkview Homes, the project near downtown on Broad Street. I had butterflies in my stomach. It was exciting to me at first because I had thought drug dealers were some of the most powerful people in the world. They had the money, the power, the clothes, the jewelry, fly cars, and they had the bitches, and they always seemed to run things around the city.

Nothing went as easy as I thought. The spot was hot as hell! There were other niggas there trying to get money, and the police were thick. The first of the month was probably the worst day to try and break into the game for a new jack like myself. I was nervous as fuck because I didn't want an undercover or a snitch to run up on me and try to figure out what I was doing and blow everything. I didn't let the other dudes know why I was there, but it became apparent very quickly. A few of the dealers I knew offered some advice, but there was no way in hell I was going to take advice from a nigga trying to get money in the same spot I was in. And you know how the old-school niggas feel about newcomers invading their spot and making it hot—they weren't trying to hear that shit!

Keke and I sat side by side on the concrete porch of a vacant apartment in Parkview, watching junkies pulling up in cars and walking past us.

"Hey, Keke, let them know we got something." I wasn't familiar with the local junkies like Keke was. Ain't no way in hell I'm going to walk up to a someone I think looks like a junkie and let them know I got rocks.

"I got this!" Keke said, jumping up from the hard ass concrete and brushing the dirt off the back of her shorts.

"What you about to do?" I asked.

"Let me handle it," she replied as she skipped off around the building. I continued to sit there with a mouth full of rocks wrapped in plastic, watching everything around me carefully and making sure I didn't miss anything. I didn't want anyone to get close to me without me seeing them first.

Keke came back and sat down beside me again and didn't say a word. An older white man appeared, looking like he had just got out of bed.

"Give it to me," she said, looking at me and holding her hand out. I spit it out in her hand, and she started off towards the man. I followed behind her. We met the dude, and he followed us to my car. Keke handed me two twenty pieces as we approached my car. I dropped the two rocks by the back tire of my car and turned around to face the man, who wasn't far behind us.

I walked towards him and said, "I dropped them by the back driver-side tire. Forty."

He handed me the balled-up money and headed towards my car, not saying a word to me or making eye contact. I unfolded the money as I walked back around the building to our post up on the porch.

"You want this back?" Keke asked as she opened her hand, showing me the piece of plastic that contained the contained the rocks.

"Naw, hold onto it," I said as I sat back on the porch to wait for my next customer.


I didn't last long in the dope game. My nerves were shot by the end of the first day. I didn't want to go to jail, and I didn't want to sell drugs anymore. Selling drugs wasn't easy. There are too many things to worry about and watch out for when you're on the streets. You can't trust any fucking body, and you have to watch your back constantly. When you're on the corner, you have to be focused on what you're doing and be cautious. You don't have a lot of chances for mistakes in the drug game. That shit is grimy as hell. One wrong move and you could end up in prison, robbed, or dead. That game is serious, and it takes the type of guts that I obviously don't possess. If it was hard back in 1993, I can't imagine what the game is like now. I have a brother in prison, and although he's not in for drugs, I can't imagine having my freedom snatched away from me all in one day. Fuck that!

I've never been into drugs myself. You would think because of the type of life that I've lived that I would have experienced some form of substance abuse, but i never have. Although I have tried drinking a few times, the last being my birthday party in 2007 in New York City, I just can't get past the taste of alcohol. I've never in my life tried anything that tasted good enough to continuously drink. Everything I've ever tried is disgusting to me so that's one good reason why I haven't been able to get into drinking.

Now as far as weed, I don't even want to try that because it might make me feel too good, and then, guess what? I'm hooked! I'm weak for anything that makes me feel good—very weak. Then I'll be a weed head and that's not cute to see, a female high with red, watery eyes and ashy lips.

At one time, I was curious to try ecstasy. I've heard so many sexual stories about E from my friends. They say it makes sex one hundred times greater than it normally feels, so, of course, I was interested in it! I only know a few people that have actually used it. I'm sure celebrities use it a lot, but I don't know which ones. The one and only reason I didn't try it was because I didn't know who to get it from and how it's supposed to look. I can't just take a pill and not know if it's really safe or it's truly what I think it is. It's not like I could take it to my doctor and ask her to confirm that it's ecstasy. My doctor and I are cool, but not that damn cool!

I was never one to frequent industry parties or become very close with industry insiders. I don't have time to hang around with people who abuse substances in their downtime. Bobby Brown is a mess. I heard he does all types of drugs. Women still seem to like him, because I heard he's still fucking a few people. Good for him, I guess, but I won't be knocking on his door to hang out anytime soon.

Smokers in the music business always confuse the hell out of me. Bun B, for instance, smokes like a chimney. I met at his video shoot in Miami and hung out with him at Kayslay's birthday party in New York City. I always thought smoking rappers and singers were odd, because you'd think they would take care of their voices. I love his music and always have, we hit it off instantly he has great southern hospitality. I would hate to see something happen to him behind smoking.

Even in my adult life, the people I'm involved with in the sports and entertainment industry don't do hard drugs, at least not that I know of. Only the urban models who smoke and drink would know who does drugs and who doesn't. I hear rappers mentioning drugs in their lyrics, but most of the time, I have no clue what they're talking about unless someone explains it to me!

Keke and I hung out all day trying to get rid of the cocaine. I didn't want to leave that block with any dope on me. At the end of the day, the dope I had left over I gave to Keke, and we made a deal to go boosting the next day, and she would just repay me that way. Yes, the money was good, but I wouldn't say that it was easy. Selling drugs is definitely a mental thing, and your mind has got to be right or else you lose, and you lose *big*. Finally, my street days were over, partly because I gained an invaluable "asset" that has been with me to this day.

# Chapter Six

During troubled times I always held down a job. No major jobs, just something to keep a little change in my pocket and help my mother with the bills since I wasn't on welfare anymore. Right out of high school I worked at Kroger in the bakery department. I loved baking and still do. I worked the morning shift for about almost 3 years until I was fired for stealing hours. Immediately after that, I started working at another grocery store called Harris Teeter. I worked there for almost 5 years in the bakery department.

One of my coworkers at Harris Teeter told me about this doctor she had visited who helped her gain weight. At the time, I was skeptical of anything or anyone that told me I could actually gain weight. My entire life I had tried everything known to mankind that I thought could help me gain weight—and nothing ever worked! I wasn't ready to completely give up on my quest to get some meat on these bones, though, so I made my appointment to see this "miracle doctor." I got on my knees the night before seeing him and prayed to God that this doctor could help me gain weight.

I was sitting in Dr. X's office, 25 miles from home. I told him how desperately I've been trying to gain weight all my life and how absolutely nothing ever worked. He gave me a list of foods that would help me gain weight, along with a prescription for a liquid appetite stimulant. I remember peanut butter and pasta being on the list, but that's about all I remember. I was hopeful when I left his office but not convinced at all.

I went home and did exactly what the doctor told me to do. I got my prescription filled and started taking it right away. Believe it or not, in less than 2 weeks, I had already started noticing a weight gain! My ass, hips, and thighs were the first parts of my body to receive this blessing. I noticed a little weight gain in my stomach area, too, but not enough to get alarmed by. It was like my ass and thighs just took off and left the rest of my body. My body started changing so fast that it seemed like it happened overnight. Everyone was noticing it too—and I mean *everybody!*

I couldn't believe that my body was developing the way it was. It was like I finally hit puberty and was becoming a real woman! I went from 120 pounds to 145 in a matter of weeks. From the waist down, it was on, baby! I couldn't stop thanking God for my blessing.

I had an ass, nice hips, and bigger thighs! You couldn't tell me shit! The men were loving me; the women wanted to be me and were all hating at the same time. I never thought being thick would make me so content with my life. Most people would say I'm very shallow for thinking like this, but I'm being real about it. What woman doesn't want to feel attractive and craved by the opposite sex? I don't consider it negative attention at all.

It's all in how you carry it. Many women would say that they want a man to be attracted to their mind and not their body. In my experience, a man doesn't see your mind until he gets to know you. All he initially sees is a beautiful, sexy, and well put-together woman. In my opinion, after your physical appearance, the mind comes which seals the deal—and that's still depending on what man you ask.

I refused to let these jealous ass females make me feel fucked up about how my body has developed. The females in Athens started rumors saying that my ass was fake and I had steroid shots in my butt. Some were even saying that I was wearing padded panties. I got into so many arguments and confrontations after I gained weight. Why is everybody fucking with me now? Do I really matter this much now?

Not all the women were haters and envious. Some would tell me how good the weight looked on me and wanted to know how I did it. My friends and family were amazed about the weight because I had always been so skinny. Everyone agreed that it looked good on me. My top stayed the same size, but my jeans went from a size 3 to a 13. I had to throw out all my jeans and buy new ones.

I noticed as I gained weight, my stomach grew a bit as well. I decided to start working out a little—not much, just enough to keep things intact. My butt outgrew everything on my body! I was literally in love with my ass! I even started doing butt exercises to shape it and get it nice and firm. Abs and butt exercises I've stayed true to for the past 10 years. And I was sticking a little cardio in there to keep the fat off my stomach.

When I was around people who didn't know me or who didn't like the attention I received, I did get hated on something terrible. It was like I won the lottery for $100 million and everyone wanted a cut! I was arguing every day with these hating ass bitches all because my ass was big and I was getting more attention than they were. It seems like no one is going to hate on you unless you're doing well in life or you're lookin' good!


A few friends of mine were exotic dancers in Atlanta, Georgia. Between you and me, I always had a negative attitude towards dancers. I thought they were the scum of the earth, and I always said that I would never disgrace myself and dance nude in front of a club full of guys. Boy, my younger self would have a heart attack if it saw my new big butt, let alone see it shakin' in a club!

My lady friends convinced me that I could make loads of money dancing with my newly developed body in Atlanta. I had the body, but was totally lacking the guts. I finally decided to take that hour drive to Atlanta just to see what was good. With my friends talking so much about the opportunities in ATL, they made the strip game seem so good and easy. They kept telling me about all the celebrities who would come in the club and pour money on them every night. They had me hyped like hell!

When we got to Atlanta, was the first time I had ever stepped foot into a strip club. Surprisingly, it wasn't as intimidating as I thought it would be. I always thought you had to be flawless to be a dancer, especially in Atlanta, but that's not the case. After seeing that most of the girls were average looking and were nowhere near perfect, it made me feel much better. I spoke with the manager of the club, and he instantly gave me a job. He didn't make me take off my clothes or dance in auditions.

The next day, I went shopping around Atlanta for shoes and outfits to dance in. I wasn't used to shoes with high heels on them like I saw the other girls wearing. I ended up buying a lime-green slingshot bathing suit and some black, low heel shoes. That same night I was in the club shaking my ass, nude.

I got used to this way of life very quickly. It was the

money and attention that I was getting that made me like it. The guys were on me! The club owners were always glad to see me because the better you looked, the better you were treated. And this was true no matter what club I danced in. The good-looking girls bring in the customers.

So now that we know how I looked, let's talk about my performance. I couldn't dance a lick! I was nothing like the females in the strip clubs, and I mean *nothing*. It took me over a year to dance half as well as most of these girls.

The very first club I danced in was Montres on the Westside of Atlanta, right across the street from the West End Mall. It was a little hole-in-the-wall club that sat right on the highway. All that separated the club from the freeway was a narrow sidewalk. If you ran out of the club too fast, you could literally get hit by a car. The parking lot was on the side of the club, and there was another lot across the highway at the Marta station, Atlanta's public transportation system.

Montres wasn't a popular club in Atlanta, but it had been there for awhile, and it was well established. It looked like a little juke joint, and if you danced there, you weren't considered a classy dancer. I didn't feel comfortable starting at a bigger club, so I settled for a lower-end place. I would work my way up as I got better and better.

I thought I would be nervous the first time, but I wasn't, and only because I wasn't the only female walking around the club half nude. I sort of blended in, I thought. The girls were nice but not very talkative. They would give you a half smile and keep it moving. I tried not to make eye contact with any of them because I know how these strip clubs feel about new girls. I came to find out later that the females can become very hateful and rude if you become popular and start getting a lot of attention, which I did. I wasn't there to make friends, so I didn't care if the girls liked me or not. My main concern was to get the men to like me, and boy, did they like me.

It was during the daytime when I started dancing at Montres, so the club wasn't really packed, but it got more crowded as the day went on. I hated getting on the stage, because I couldn't dance, and that's when all the attention was on me. I'm sure the girls laughed at me, and maybe the men, too, but I just couldn't get my body to move like those other dancers. It was extremely difficult to learn as I went, but I was determined to do it.

I would love to sit in the club and watch the girls dance on stage. They moved so fluidly and on beat. They had me mesmerized. The way they moved their bodies was simply amazing. I never knew a person's body could jiggle, bounce, and bend like that. It took practice, and no person could just walk in a club and expect to dance like that their first night.

I made maybe $200 or $300 the first night. That was great money to me, knowing that I barely made that at the supermarket in an entire week. I was happy as hell! The customers seemed to like me, and the manager asked me before I left if I would be back the next day. My first hustle in the strip game turned out to be a positive one. It took me a while to learn how to dance like the other dancers, and the reason it took me so long is because I only danced part-time for the first 2 years. I was still working at the supermarket in Athens full-time. I couldn't drive to Atlanta every day, usually only on the weekends. After work every day, I would go home and practice my dancing in the mirror. I was determined to be one of the best dancers in the club.

While dancing, I got my first taste of the sports and entertainment industry. I saw some of the local rappers in the strip clubs in Atlanta, including Kilo and Raheem the Dream, but I also remember seeing Professor X of Public Enemy, Kriss Kross, Warren Sapp, K-Ci and JoJo, Jim Jones, Lil Wayne, Usher, Vin Baker, Steve Francis, Shaq, and too many more to name. I rarely danced for celebrities because when they showed up, I was already with high-paying customers and had little interest in messing around with the dancers who were viciously competing for attention. I wouldn't risk sacrificing my game just to be able to say I sat with a big name.

I did dance for Allen Iverson. The club was called Moet, in Philly. It was a nice club and very tastefully decorated, with mirror-lined walls and three stages. It was Friday night, and I was on stage doing my thing. Next thing you know, there was a big commotion at the front door. I never jumped off the stage to see what was going on because if someone was fighting, they may have a gun. I continued to dance and before long, Allen Iverson appeared through the door with about 10 other men. Everyone was hysterical and acting crazy like they had never seen a big name before.

I'm not going to lie; I was a little excited myself. I wasn't a basketball fan, but I knew exactly who he was, and I've always thought he was incredibly sexy. The club owners rushed him and his entourage straight to the VIP room, and it seemed like almost, if not all, the dancers followed.

When it was my time to leave the stage, I went to the dressing room to freshen up and get myself together. After I finished, I came out and went to the VIP room to see if there was some money to be made, because I didn't have any clients waiting for a dance yet. When I got to their room, it was so dark I could barely see my hands in front of me. I stood around, scoping out the scene. The girls were all over the niggas. They were sitting in their laps and drinking. None of the girls were actually dancing; it was more like they were there to party.

Finally, I made eye contact with Al, who didn't have a chick in his lap. He was sitting there enjoying his drink and the music. While his boys were loudly enjoying themselves, he sat quietly. He motioned for me to come and sit down beside him, and I did. He asked me my name and where was I from and what was I doing in Philly. I answered his questions, then he asked me if I wanted something to drink and I politely turned him down. He asked me if I felt like dancing.

I got up, took off my clothes, and started dancing to the next song that came on. I was so nervous that I couldn't even dance right. I was offbeat, and I couldn't get my moves together for nothing! As he sat and watched me, it made me more and more nervous. I was wishing so bad that anybody or anything would distract him from looking at me. I wanted to be perfect at that moment just because it was him.

After a few songs, he asked me what he owed me because he and his boys were about to bounce. He paid me and gave me a hug. He also gave me his number, told me to call him the next day, and he and his boys bounced.

Sometimes celebrities spent money, but most of the time they didn't. I could make more money from my regular customers than from these celebrities. I wasn't familiar with most of the NFL and NBA players anyway. I came to find out who they were because I would overhear the girls talking excitedly in the dressing room about who was in the club, and then I still wouldn't know what they looked like to match a name to a face.

Most of the chicks would flock to these celebrities in the club, but I wouldn't. I would treat them like I would any other customer. If they weren't spending any money, I wasn't going to be a groupie and sit with them all night, hoping that maybe they would spend some money—which was never guaranteed. As long as a customer was spending money, I would sit with him all night long. All money is the same to me, whether it comes from a celebrity or not, but some girls don't seem to understand this.

Atlanta is known as the place you want to be if you're an exotic dancer. If you're looking to visit a strip club and you're deciding what city to visit that has the girls with the biggest asses, the best dancers, the niggas who really spend money, totally nude clubs that still sell alcohol and the widest variety of black-owned and -operated joints, then believe me when I tell you Atlanta, Georgia, is your destination!

Now, I must warn you that not all the girls are shapely and pretty, so forget what you've been told. I know you may hear that Atlanta is "where it's at," but you have some boo-boos there, too, just like any other city.

Butt injections are on the rise and growing at an alarming rate. I've never in my life seen so many women getting their asses blown up! I saw a few of my fellow dancers back in the day go and get butt shots. You have a lot of phat asses in Atlanta. A lot of them are not real and therefore look weird and are shaped oddly. Don't get me wrong, I have no problem at all with fake anything. But when the shit looks horrible or "unreal," then it's funny as hell!

In the last few years, I've made my way back to most of the clubs in Atlanta just to visit. I've seen some asses that looked sad. How in the hell can you weigh 125 pounds and carrying an ass bigger than mine? The thighs don't match, the legs don't match, and the waist doesn't match! The shit looks like a watermelon walking on two pretzels! Come on, girls, if you're going to get ass shots, try to make it proportional to your body. And stop trying to outdo the next female. Every girl in the strip club wants to be known for the one with the biggest ass—and bigger isn't always better if your shit looks deformed. I'm not in any way talking against butt shots, so close your mouth before you start hating. Shit, if my ass was small or nearly flat, I would be the first bitch in line trying to get some ass shots … believe that shit!

I knew a few girls who even went to the extent of getting the injections in their hips and their breasts. One girl who went and got hip injections looked as if someone glued two brown mounds on each side of her. It looked terrible. I knew several girls who were getting the injections in their breasts. One girl had to have her breast removed because she fell ill from an infection caused by that.

Girls e-mail me all the time, asking for advice on where to get butt injections. I never respond to any of those e-mails because for one, my ass is not fake and I know that's why females ask me where to get it done. People can say for the rest of their life that my butt is fake, and all I will do is laugh. They want my butt to be fake so badly. You can't find my ass in a doctor's office or from a needle, because it is all real. In my opinion, all most of these females need to do is gain a little weight and exercise. You can always make your butt bigger by exercising and building the muscles in your booty. That's what I did, and it works. Most black females hate to workout, and believe me, I'm one of them, but I suck it up to maintain!

Stripping wasn't easy because after a while, it was like any of my other jobs. I worked hard for my payout. It was still fun and very interesting because every night was different. Even if I had a daughter, I don't know if I would tell her not to dance if she wanted to. I don't think it's a bad thing to frequent strip clubs, as long as you know how to handle being around alcohol and nude women. Not everyone can control themselves when they have these two temptations presented in front of them at the same time. Not all women can handle the flow of alcohol and readily available drugs, not to mention the men who use and abuse substances and treat the dancers with disrespect. If I thought my daughter had a weak mind and was easily misled, I would beg her not to dance.

# Chapter Seven

While I was dancing at Foxy Lady on Moreland Avenue in Atlanta, I met a big-time drug dealer named Chris. Chris was thick, almost fat, about 6'3" and dark-skinned with a mouth full of gold teeth. He was really cute and a little arrogant. He would come in the club at least two or three times a week and spend loads of money at the bar and on the dancers. All the dancers knew him, and you could tell by the talk in the dressing room that he had close relationships in the past with a few of the girls.

One Friday night he came into the club. Foxy Lady was jumping as usual, and I was working on my grind. Chris walked in a little after midnight with his homeboys that always tagged along with him. Like always, they spent crazy money. Every girl who went on stage was sure to get paid when Chris was in there.

I was always nervous when I hit the stage; even though I had become a fluent dancer, I felt people were watching me closely and judging. Some of the dancers would even laugh and joke about how I danced, but in the end, I didn't care. I would still make just as much money on stage as the females who could really dance. I would love dancing to 8Ball and MJG. Later, I met them in Memphis at a party. They were incredibly kind, old-school men. I wonder how much those dancers would have hated on me if they knew who I would become.

When I got on stage that night, Chris and his boys showered the platform with dollar bills. Bills were flying everywhere. Before I left the stage, Chris came up and whispered in my ear to come and see him when I finished, and I agreed. I grabbed up my money from the floor and went off to the dressing room to freshen up and organize my bills.

After I was finished in the dressing room, I went back out to the floor to find Chris. He and his boys were chillin' in a group, and there were four or five girls giving them table dancing. I sat down next to Chris and thanked him for the money on stage. He laughed and said it was nothing. I sat there and talked with him about 20 minutes. We exchanged numbers, then I got up and went back to work.

When Foxy Lady closed for the night, Chris called me and asked if I wanted to meet him for breakfast, and I said sure. We met up at a diner in downtown Atlanta and ate and talked. He convinced me to stay in Atlanta after we finished eating because it was late and I was sleepy as hell. He got a room, and we stayed the night together. We didn't have sex the first night, but it did come after the second time I spent the night with him.

We became very cool, and I really liked him. He trapped over off Boulder Crest, so I would often hang out in the trap with him. I wasn't naïve or crazy. I knew it wasn't safe to be there with him, but after a few months, I was so wrapped up into him that I couldn't think responsibly. He was taking me shopping and giving me jewelry. I didn't even have to go and dance if I didn't feel like it. Chris was full of himself, and he liked to brag about the money he made, and he sure didn't mind spending it. He was young and felt invincible. He was sort of loud, too, but he wasn't a hard person to deal with. I think I was more into him than he was into me. Girls love dudes like him, so I know when I wasn't in Atlanta, he would deal with girls much more fly than I. I was just a little country girl from Athens compared to some of the girls in Atlanta.

One Sunday afternoon, we headed toward Candler Road in Decatur to have a bracelet fixed that he had given me. He knew a friend of his that worked at the Candler Road Flea Market that would fix the bracelet. When we got there, the flea market hadn't opened yet. He mentioned that he had a homeboy that lived two streets over that he had to see, so he asked me to drive him over there. We headed out, and I pulled up in front of the house and parked. He got out and said he would be right back and it wouldn't take long. He went in the house, and I sat there listening to music and watching these little hood dudes hanging on the corner in front of me at the stop sign. The street was full of boys walking back and forth past me, staring as they went by. I didn't pay as much attention to them as I did my music.

A few minutes later, I saw Chris coming out of the house and walking back towards my car. As he reached for the door handle, two men who were hanging around the intersection behind me ran up to the car and slammed a gun into the back of Chris's head. I started yelling and screaming for help. One of the men ran over to the driver's side of the car and demanded that I shut the fuck up, get out of the car, start walking away and not look back. I was so confused, but I did what I was told and didn't say a word. As I started walking, I could hear them behind me trying to crank my car, but the car kept stalling for some strange reason. I heard Chris begging for his life, and I started crying.

*I can't leave Chris like this*, I thought. I turned around to walk back to help Chris, and the man who had initially told me to leave saw that I had disobeyed him. He met me and hit my head with the gun.

"Bitch, do what I said!"

I started screaming for my life and fell to the ground. I didn't fall because of the blow to the head, but because I was so full of fear that I couldn't stand any longer. I just crumbled to the ground. By this time, the people in the house came out shooting pistols. The carjackers took off running. I lay in the street crying and screaming, more concerned about Chris's condition than my own. I didn't know if he was dead or alive because I couldn't see him. He was lying on the other side of the car on the curb where I had parked earlier. I kept asking where Chris was, and the neighbor who lifted me up off the street told me the paramedics were on their way.

I couldn't believe what had just happened to me. I couldn't stop shaking as the neighbor led me into his house. They had taken Chris into the house that I was parked in front of, so I couldn't see how badly he was hurt. I asked the neighbor how Chris was again, and he assured me that Chris was okay and he would be fine. He asked me if I was alright, and I told him I was, but I still couldn't stop crying or shaking. I just sat on the floor, dazed and crying. I heard the ambulance outside, and I saw the lights flashing, but I couldn't get up. I was glued to the floor.

Finally, one of the paramedics came in to check me out. I wasn't hit hard enough that I felt like I had to go to the hospital. I asked the paramedic how Chris was doing, and he said he was already in the ambulance, and he would be okay, but he had to go to the hospital. I got up, thanked the homeowner for being so helpful and kind, and I followed the paramedic outside to check on Chris and let him know I would follow him to the emergency room.

The left side of Chris's face was unrecognizable. His eye was swollen, and his face was bloody and bruised. He told me he was alright, but I know he really wasn't. The two guys had robbed him of over ten grand and took all the jewelry he was wearing. I told him I was going to follow him to the hospital, and I did. When I got to the hospital, his mother, sister, and a large, ghetto female were in the waiting room. Come to find out, the third woman was supposedly Chris's girlfriend.

When she found out who I was and why I was there, you could tell she didn't approve. She never said anything to me, but she was loud and acting like she was so upset about what had happened to Chris. She kept saying things to make me know that Chris was her man and that they were really close. His mother and sister didn't talk much outside of asking me what had happened. As I sat and talked to them, the doctor came over and told us we could go back to see Chris. I told them they could go first and I would go in after they came out. The three of them went back while I waited.

After a few minutes, they came out and his mother told me that Chris wanted to see me. I could tell that the ghetto chick was hot with anger, but at this point, I didn't give a shit how she felt. I almost lost my life over this nigga, so nothing matters now.

I went in the room, and Chris was smiling when I walked in. He was in very good spirits, considering what we had just gone through a few hours earlier. He tried to explain to me that the ghetto chick was not his girlfriend. She was someone he used to date that wouldn't leave him alone. I told him it didn't matter, and I didn't care to talk about that because I didn't believe him anyway. He said he would be discharged from the hospital that night and asked if I stay with him.

I told him my family was worried because I had told them what had happened and they wanted me to come home. He understood. I told him I would call him when I got home. I left the hospital and got in my car, and I never called Chris again. He called me a few times after that night, but I never answered the phone.

It was at least 2 months after that before I would even think about going to Atlanta. That ordeal was too scary and real. It was like something you see on TV, and I couldn't believe I was involved in it and still living to tell about it. I had been rough after high school, but I had never in my life been attacked so viciously by men. Fighting some trippin' females is nothing like having a gun pointed at you while you're with the one you love.

The police department from Atlanta called me a couple of times, but I told them I wasn't interested in talking to them about it because they would never find the carjackers. What the fuck do the police care about one drug dealer robbing another drug dealer anyway? They don't give a damn about that type of shit. That's what they want, for us to kill each other so they won't have to deal with the bullshit.

When I finally went back to Atlanta, I went straight to Foxy Lady and I didn't stop for anything, not even gas. When I got to the club, everyone had found out about what had happened to Chris and me. Everybody wanted to hear my side of the story. I didn't want to relive that time again, so I told everyone who asked that I didn't want to talk about it. The word on the street and in the club was that I was the reason Chris got robbed. People were saying that I'm the one who had orchestrated the entire hit and that's why I hadn't been back to work. I couldn't believe what I was being accused of! How on earth could it be my fault when it wasn't my idea to go to this house or that side of town? That was all Chris's idea, and he knew it.

I started trying to explain myself to everyone at the club. I didn't know if they believed me or not, but I knew the truth and so did Chris. As the night went on, I kept wondering if Chris really thought that I had something to do with that. A couple of hours before the club closed that night, Chris walked through the door with his boys. I was dancing in the corner for a dude, so I couldn't just leave and go to the dressing room. I tried to pretend that his presence didn't bother me, but it really did, and the guy I was dancing for could tell. He tapped me on the arm and asked me if I was okay. I said "Yes" in an unsure way. Chris and his homies took a table right at the stage in front of where I was dancing and started popping bottles. He threw money like he normally did. I guess he was trying to prove to everyone that he still had money and he was still that nigga, regardless of what happened to him a few months ago.

I tried not to pay him any attention as I continued working that night. I caught him watching me most of the night, but I played it off like I didn't notice. I guess someone had called him and informed him that I was back at work and he wanted to come and harass me. As the night went on, Chris couldn't deal with me ignoring him anymore. He walked up to me while I was dancing for my customer and poured an entire bottle of champagne over my head until the bottle was empty. He set the bottle on the table and walked away. I took off behind him, and the security guard grabbed me and took me to the dressing room. I was yelling and cursing as they tried to keep me inside the room.

"How in the hell are y'all going to grab *me* but not *him*?" I yelled. He spent so much money in the club that they wouldn't dare make him leave. That goes to show how much they cared for their girls. I washed up and got dressed because the club was now closed. All the girls were talking in the dressing room about what had just happened, but I said nothing. After I was dressed, I went outside. Chris and his boys were standing outside chatting in the parking lot with some other guys. I went straight to my car, and Chris came up behind me and told me he was sorry. He told me how hurt and abandoned he felt when I never called him again, and he felt that I didn't have any feelings for what had happened to him.

I explained that I did care, but I was shaken at the same time. I told him how I turned around and tried to come back and help him after one of the dudes had put a pistol in my face and told me to leave. He asked me to go with him that night, and without even thinking about anything, I said yes. I followed him to his apartment, which wasn't in an area that I would consider safe. It was in the middle of the hood. I was nervous the entire night and didn't sleep well at all. I remember waking up every 15 minutes, looking around and wishing that daylight would hit soon.

Finally the sun came up. I got up and didn't even wash my face or brush my teeth. I got in my car and told Chris I had something to do and I would call him in a few hours. He said okay and gave me a kiss. I left the apartment complex, and I never saw it or Chris again.

# Chapter Eight

By the time I was fired from the supermarket, I was dancing at my third strip club, Club Nikki VIP, on Stewart Avenue. After almost 5 years at the supermarket, I was terminated for physically assaulting my manager. We were arguing one morning, and I threw a box at her.

Montres was closed down for some reason. One day I came to work, and a padlock was on the door. Club Nikki was a little different from the first two clubs I had danced in. Montres and Foxy Lady were never considered top-notch joints. They both fell at the bottom of the list when it came to exclusivity, popularity, the quality of the girls, the amount of money that the club makes, and the amount the customers spends. At Nikki's, the girls looked better, the club was more upscale and cleaner, and it was considered one of the exclusive, more popular clubs in Atlanta at that time, and all the local drug dealers and wealthy men hung out here.

You could tell which females were the top moneymakers by the cars they drove. They had the brand-new Navigators, Expeditions, and Lexus SUVs. These females could dance, and they had some tricks for your ass! And when I say "tricks," I truly mean sellin' tail. I quickly realized why this club was so popular. To make some real money at Club Nikki, you had to be down for more than just dancing. When I realized this, I decided in no way was I down for that type of shit! I had never even thought to engage in any form of prostitution.

I studied these females for a while. Those who were tricking were the girls who drove the high-end luxury cars, who wore the expensive clothes, who carried the big Gucci & Fendi bags, and who looked like money. These females weren't beautiful, and they weren't ugly. They were all average, nice-looking females with lots of ass. It's not fair to say that all the dancers were tricking, because they weren't. But the ones who were had no shame in their game.

After being there for a while and seeing the type of money these women were making and how all the dudes with money would flock to them, my mind gradually changed. I started following in the footsteps of the top girls. I didn't have my 9 to 5 job anymore, so I needed this money. Once again, I had the desire to fit in and wanted to be one of the "top bitches" driving the high-end cars and living well.

I was too scared to sell pussy in the club, like most of the girls were doing (this was probably the safest way of doing it, too), so I started setting up dates for after the club. The going price for sex at that time was between $300 and $500. That price would get a guy one nut. I wasn't sucking dick, so I lost a few dates because of that. Most guys prefer a head job without a condom, and I refused to put a raw penis in my damn mouth. On top of that, I've had bad nightmares of trying to give a trick some head and his balls were musty and sweaty and I vomited all over him.

I hated tricking. I was disgusted when a client would try to kiss me in my mouth, suck my breasts, or try to give me oral sex. I've always believed that a trick shouldn't want to do those things. I felt like my only job was to bend over and let a nigga hit me from the back, he nuts, I wash up, and I leave. I hated when they wanted to lay and make love and talk instead of just fucking and getting it done with. Time was money! Get your nut and get the fuck on!

I would never trick with a man that I didn't become familiar with inside the club first. I would dance for the dude and make money off him in the club. We would talk and get to know a little about each other and then maybe set something up for after the club. I would have to feel comfortable with a man first, and I think I'm a pretty good judge of character.

The very first time was with a man named Erik. He was a goofy nerd. He was light-skinned, slim, and much shorter than I, and he just seemed to me like he couldn't harm a fly. Those were the types of guys that I would stick to when it came to tricking. The men who weren't too loud in the club and who were bashful. They would always sit in the dark corner of the club, like they were ashamed to be in such a place. They always spent money and were always nice.

I tricked with Erik a few times. I would always get my money up front, no matter how cool I was with someone. We would go to a hotel, even though we would only be there for at most an hour. I would get my money when we walked into the room. Then I would get undressed, leaving my shirt on most of the time because I didn't want a trick trying to kiss or touch my chest. It gave me the creeps.

I would get on all fours so they could hit it from the back, but for some reason, most guys wanted me to lie on my back so they could get on top of me. I was always told that hitting it from the back with an ass like mine would make them cum too quickly, and they wanted their time to last as long as possible. After they got their first nut, I would rush to the bathroom to wipe off the sweat that would drop off them onto me, and wipe off anywhere that I came into contact with them, especially my privates. I would scrub my pussy so hard I was close to a good waxing! I would be so disgusted when the ordeal was over that I felt like throwing up.

Sometimes the men would ask for a second round. I will admit the second time with the same person was always better than the first time with a new nigga. I would get my money and lie back on the bed and go another round. This time was always longer, of course, but never too long. After I finally left the hotel, I would jump in my Expedition and lock my doors as if someone were chasing me.

Tricking wasn't hard work, but it was very stressful and emotionally exhausting. The only thing that made me feel okay about what I had just done was the money I had in my purse. Almost a grand for a little over an hour of laying on my back, not to even mention the money I made in the club earlier that night.

Even though I had money, I often still felt like the dude I tricked with got the better end of the stick. They got to use me to fulfill their pleasures, and they knew they could any time—as long as they had cash. After tricking for a few months, I was fed up and couldn't take it anymore. No money was worth an unattractive, fat, sweaty, and jacked-up nigga lying on top of me trying to make love and kissing me on my neck! I danced at Nikki's a few more weeks, and I bounced.

I went to the Body Tap on Marietta Street next. At the time, Body Tap wasn't as popular as Nikki's, but it was a lot more laid-back. It wasn't an environment where the guys expected sex when they walked in the door. Body Tap was the first club I chose to work the day shift full-time. Of course, there is more money to make on the night shift at any strip club, but on night shift, the girls are harder to work with, you have more fights, the dressing room is overcrowded, and driving late at night was beginning to take a toll on me.

On day shift, I would work from noon to around seven o'clock. I was bringing home between $400 and $600 a day, so I was satisfied with that, and I was usually home by 8:30 every night. I had my own condo, a new Expedition, and money in the bank. I was pretty comfortable with my life at that time. I was dating, but didn't really have a stable relationship. After almost 2 years, I started looking for newer and better places to dance.

I left Body Tap on a mission to find more lucrative clubs. Who knew that after setting off, I would never dance in Atlanta again? I don't even know why I danced in Atlanta as long as I did. Maybe because Atlanta is a known challenge to take on if you wanted to make it in the stripping game. I had to prove to myself that if I could succeed in the Atlanta strip clubs, any other city would be a drop in the bucket … and it was.

South Carolina was my next stop, and Charleston would be the city. Money, money, and more money! Who would have thought those country boys in Charleston could spend like that? Eight hundred dollars a night was easy to make there. I was balling! I would leave South Carolina on a Sunday, headed back home with over $2,000 in my pocket for just 2 days of work. I started dancing all over South Carolina: Columbia, Dillon, Greenville, Spartanburg, Orangeburg, Neeses, and Florence.

South Carolina was the shit! Fuck Atlanta with all those damn rules! In Atlanta, you had to have a license to dance, you couldn't dance at multiple clubs with that one license, you had to work 7 or 8 hours or else you had to pay a fine, and tipping out (what you pay to dance at the club) was getting more and more expensive. I moved around South Carolina for well over a year, making money and going home during the week.

I started dating a man from Orangeburg name Maurice. He owned one of the local clubs that I frequented. I stayed at his house during the weekend and only went back to Athens to check on my condo and pack clean clothes every few weeks. I began to like staying in South Carolina. South Carolina was a little slow and behind the times, but I needed the laid-back atmosphere. Maurice and my relationship never got to a serious point because I didn't feel like I could permanently be with a guy who runs a strip club, and he felt he could never be serious with a stripper. With us both being in the entertainment industry, we knew all the bullshit that goes on in the clubs, so I don't think we ever fully trusted each other.

I haven't ever met a club owner in my days of dancing that didn't fuck the girls. I'm not saying that Maurice did for sure, but why wouldn't he? He is a man, and he likes pussy just like all other men. Maurice and I really didn't have a life outside the club with each other. On the days he wasn't at his club, he would lay around the house or maybe drive to Columbia on Sundays to hang out at the clubs there. Our relationship was a little boring to me; there was no real excitement. He was older than I so he was sort of set in his ways. I used to fuss with him because I wanted to take vacations and go out and do things, and he would always promise me we would start doing more, but he never kept his promises.

I broke up with him, more than once, and he would promise me to do better if I came back. He would be more active in the relationship for a while, but eventually things would go right back to being boring. I got sick and tired of being bored, so I broke up with him for the last time. We were still having sex after the breakup because I still had feelings for him, but I wouldn't dedicate all my energy to an otherwise boring relationship. He became borderline obsessive, showing up at the clubs I was dancing in, and he'd e-mail and call me like crazy.

Early one Saturday morning, I got up at 5 a.m. to call Maurice. He was just leaving his club and was on his way home. He said he would stop to pick up some breakfast first and then go home. I was in Columbia at the time. He told me he was coming to Columbia later that day and he would call me when he was on his way.

"Cool," I said, and he hung up. I noticed something wasn't right about that phone call. He was too eager to get off the phone, and any other time, he would talk to me until he was home and in the bed. I felt a little suspicious, so I got up and put on some sweatpants and a top, brushed my teeth and hair, and sped out of the house, jumped in my truck, and headed to Orangeburg. I needed to see why he was in such a hurry to get off the phone. My hands were sweaty, and my heart was racing. I just *knew* he was up to some bullshit! Even though I had "officially" left him and started dating someone else, I still felt uneasy about the idea that he was sleeping around while still somewhat involved with me.

I jumped on Interstate 26 East headed to his house. It normally took 30 or 40 minutes to get to his house in Orangeburg from Columbia, but I swear I got there in 15 minutes, and I don't remember anything I passed!

The sun was coming up when I pulled up at his house. His Mercedes was in the yard, so I knew he had made it home. I didn't pull in his driveway because I didn't want him to know I was there. I parked in a neighbor's yard and shut my truck off. My heart was beating so fast I actually thought I was going to pass out, but my blood was pumping like crazy, and I was ready for anything or anyone that wasn't right!

I quietly walked onto his front porch and peeped into the little square window on the front of his door. *Goddamn muthafucka!* What did I see? A candle lit inside a small glass and a small, patent leather, cheap ass, churchgoing grandmother-looking purse sitting on the coffee table beside the candle. I could only see the right side of the living room where the TV, sofa, and table sat. I didn't know where the bitch or Maurice were. I assumed they were in the bedroom, and just the thought made me go insane!

Without even thinking, I rushed the front door and the entire door—frame and all—cracked open and wooden pieces went flying everywhere. I had destroyed everything that was holding the door together. It scared the fuck out of me because I didn't know that I could cause that much damage to a house. As I fell through the door onto the floor in the living room, I saw Maurice jump up from his computer in his underwear. He watched me jump up and sprint off down through the kitchen to his bedroom. As I got halfway down the hall, he tried to grab me and ripped my sweatpants, but I didn't give a damn. I wanted to know *who* was in his bedroom! When I made it to the door of his bedroom, I stopped in my tracks and just stared.

Two strippers, dressed in their T-shirts only, were sitting in his bed counting the money they had made that night. Obviously, they had heard the commotion as I made my way to them, because they had already started screaming and folding their bodies in the corner of the bed in terror, not knowing what the hell was going on.

By this time, Maurice had grabbed me around my waist.

"Get the fuck out of my house! What's wrong with you? How in the fuck you going to come and break down my door? *I'm* not your nigga anymore! You left me, and we're not together anymore!" he shouted.

He protested over and over. I just cried as he followed

me to the front door, which was still standing wide open. I stopped and looked back at him.

"How can you talk to me like this?" I said in a weak voice as tears poured down my face.

"Get the fuck out! And you better pay for my door before I call the police on you!" he said in an uncaring way. Just the way he was talking to me was killing me inside; he used a tone like I wasn't shit to him. Not to mention the strippers on the bed were listening to everything and were probably laughing at me making a pure fool out of myself. I finally left, and he slammed what was left of the door behind me.

I was so hurt that all I could do was sit in my truck, crying like there was no tomorrow. I changed my number and vowed never to deal with him again. Unfortunately, after all this, he became a full-blown stalker. E-mailing me, sitting out in front of my place, coming to the clubs I was dancing in, all the time trying to explain why the girls were at his place and apologizing for talking to me in a fucked-up way. I know I was wrong for going to his house and breaking down his door, because in all honesty, I did leave him for someone else. But I felt like he didn't have to handle it the way that he did. He knew I still cared for him, and I knew he still cared for me.

And again, I started back having sex with him. I couldn't help it! Relationships are like bad addictions sometimes. It didn't last too long after that because he couldn't see me like he wanted to, and we fussed more than we fucked. I changed my number again, and we never dealt with each other after that.

By mid-2003 and into 2004, I had begun to travel more and more. I migrated to North Carolina. I danced in Greensboro, Winston-Salem, Charlotte, Raleigh, and Durham. Yes, I made my mark everywhere I went. I didn't have any female friends, and I didn't make any either. Most of the females in the clubs didn't talk to me. Every now and then, there would be another woman who I would be social with, but I never brought the club home. If I met you at the club, then that's where it would stay. I didn't trust any ladies and no niggas. I was a female traveling alone to places I had never been or heard of before. I knew I had to be careful and cautious of my surroundings and the people I dealt with.

Having a nice face, a flat stomach, and a big round ass were an advantage, no matter what city or state I danced in. I was always greeted with smiles and open arms by the club owners and staff when I would come to dance at their club. The females hated to see me coming! When I would walk through the dressing room door, they would start scrambling like roaches to get dressed so they could get on the dance floor and make them some money before I got to the dance floor. They would make little comments like, "Oh, shit, here comes Big Booty Tasty. I know we won't make any money tonight!" I would simply ignore them and get dressed.

The biggest haters in the clubs were always the females who didn't make any money and always tricked for a living. They would always get mad at me because I possessed ambition and I wasn't lazy. I learned how to make real money in the strip game. My rules were simple: 1. Always stay new, never dance at one club too long; 2. Work out and always stay in shape; 3. Always look different and stand out from the other dancers; 4. Don't sit around and gossip with the dancers—work, work, work! 5. Keep it business. If a dude wants to talk, let him know you're there to work and you'll chat with him later if he's not tipping!

I had special privileges when I traveled versus just dancing at one club all the time. Because I traveled so much, I was always the "fresh face" or the "new girl" at the clubs. Club owners would even call me and ask me to come back to their club, and some would even pay me to be there. Any time there were big events or celebrities and athletes that were planning on being at the club, the owner would always want me there to be one of the main dancers for the night.

The celebrities were mainly the local athletes, local drug dealers with status, or local rappers who were trying to get into the industry. I never knew any of these people by name or face because they were local celebrities, or "hood celebrities." They would spend pretty decent money and would be, for the most part, easy to deal with. They would always rent out the VIP rooms and have a few girls in there dancing nonstop. After the money stopped, I would leave and go work in another part of the club. If you just sat around, you knew eventually they would start asking you what was up after the club, and I didn't want to even hear that shit! I would give them a hug or kiss on the cheek and thank them. I'd always keep it moving.

My strip club game became tighter and tighter as the months turned into years. I started traveling with my sewing machine. I would make my own costumes to dance in. Girls used to ask me to make them outfits, but I really didn't like associating with the dancers because it might have distracted me from stacking paper. During those times and still today, I don't easily trust people.

I worked my way from the Southeast to the Dirty South to the Southwest, dancing in Augusta, Macon, and Savannah, Birmingham, Jackson, New Orleans, Houston, Jacksonville, and then back to the East Coast, headed north to Portsmouth, D.C., Baltimore, Philly, Detroit, and Memphis. My goal at that time was to dance at every black strip club on this side of the map, as long as it wasn't too far to drive. I would go to each city and stay approximately 2 weeks and then go back home. I would stay home for a few weeks until I was broke, and then I would go to the next city. I did this for the last 2 or 3 years of my dancing career.

If I had to say what cities I made the most money in, they would have to be Baltimore, Charleston, and Houston.

I frequented these cities the most because of the profit. I would always research my clubs on the Internet before visiting the city. Then I would call the club owner up, ask what the qualifications and rules were to dance at their club, and I was off to work. Some clubs were totally nude, some were just topless, some were lap dancing, some were just table dancing, and some let you fuck in the club.

The states that were notorious for letting girls turn tricks in the clubs were Alabama, North Carolina, Tennessee, and Texas. Not all of the clubs in these states allowed this, and in other states, the joints that offered it were few and far between. Those clubs were always challenging because every guy that came in the club assumed that all the females were down for prostitution, and this simply wasn't true. You had females charging between $40 and $60 for head. Some of the shit I saw in some of these clubs was just disgusting. There was this one female named Lick in North Carolina who would stick a tall can of beer all the way in her pussy and let the beer shoot out. Then I would see girls letting niggas dig their fingers up their assholes and pussies.

I had never seen a dildo in my life until I started traveling to South Carolina. Girls would be on stage using toys and masturbating. Atlanta has some of the strictest rules because you would never see this type of shit there. I was exposed to all sorts of behavior in other states, especially North and South Carolina, bar none. The going price for pussy in these two states was also between $40 and $60, and that's for

for everything! I would see some girls go in the VIP to fuck a dozen or more times a night. I'd just turn my head and keep it moving. There was no shame in my game, but my game was tighter than most, and I knew what I was capable of collecting without getting down and dirty.

# Chapter Nine

I was sick of Athens. I was born there, grew up there, went to school there, got into fights there, dated guys there, and had gone to jail a few times there. I knew most of the people, and they knew me, and lord knows they had an opinion of me. How much can one take? I was ready to get the hell out of Dodge in search of new faces, new places, and definitely, new opportunities!

Tyrone was a good man. I met him in April of 2001, but we didn't start dating until 6 or 7 months later. I was a stripper when I met him. He was bashful and looked younger than his age. He was a little shorter than I and wore glasses on occasion. I met him at a motorcycle show at the local park. He didn't speak much when I first met him. He was with a group of other bikers that were loud and very vocal.

My attention was drawn to him because his demeanor was the total opposite of what I was normally attracted to. He definitely wasn't the type of guy I was used to dating. Back home, I picked out men who were in and out of jail, sold drugs, hustled, were very confrontational, never worked a 9 to 5, were bad tempered, and would slap a bitch or nigga in a minute.

I was dealing with a totally different breed this time. It was very refreshing, something I needed in my life at that time. I could tell the very first time I talked to him on the phone that he was raised in a good home. He didn't curse, he didn't smoke, he never used derogatory names when addressing women, and he just was plain respectable. I knew I wasn't the type of girl he was used to either. I had seen pictures of some of his exes, and they were all light-skinned. They didn't wear weaves and didn't have a noticeable shape, which was, of course, the total opposite of me.

Tyrone was never a person who shopped much or was into expensive things. He was a very modest person and one of the sweetest people I had ever met. He was there when I would come home from being on the road for 2 or 3 weeks. What else could I need or ask for?


While dancing at Norma Jeans in Baltimore in September of 2004, I met a guy in the club who hooked me up with this awesome photographer that lived in D.C. For no reason at all, I just wanted to take some sexy, nonnude swimsuit photos of myself to give to Tyrone and have for myself.

A week later, the photographer drove up to my hotel in Baltimore, and we shot photos all that day in my hotel room. I had purchased outfits and swimwear from the local mall, and I did my own makeup and hair. The shoot went well. I was very pleased with the photos. The photographer said that he would mail a disk to me in South Carolina in a few days, and he left. I don't even remember if he charged me for the shoot or not. If he did, it wasn't much. He called me about a week later when I was back home and told me my disk was in the mail. I was anxious to see how my mini photo shoot turned out.

By the time I received the disk in the mail, the photographer phoned me again to inform me that the photos he had taken of me were floating all over the Internet.

*"WHAT?"* I thought I was hearing things! How in the hell did my photos get online? I was heated. I lost it. He tried to explain how he had taken two of the photos and placed them on his photography Web site, and the next thing he knew, they had spread like wildfire.

I felt like he was lying to me. I thought he and his friend, the one who had referred him, had purposely posted my images all over the Internet, and they were trying to sabotage me. I told Tyrone, and he was furious. I went online, and my photos were on every message board that existed. I was so upset and considered suing the photographer.

I went from one site to another, looking at my photos and the people commenting on them. I was amazed at how people were reacting. They were really going crazy over my photos, like they had never seen a woman with a big ass in their life. Everybody wanted to know who this thick, chocolate, big booty cutie was.

I knew I was a sensation in the strip clubs, but was I really as hot as these people were pretending that I was? For the next month or so, I kept watching my images closely on the Internet as they grew more and more popular. I can understand why men would lose their minds in a strip club because the women are nude and they are up close and personal. But how in the world can you be so mesmerized by a female you see in a photo?

The response I got on the Internet was so crazy that I decided to e-mail some of my photos to the people who really knew what was hot and what wasn't: the urban modeling agencies and the magazine photographers. If anyone knew who was hot, it would be them. I went through a few of my *BlackMen* magazines I had at home and skimmed through the pages to see who was responsible to shoot the photos. I got the names and e-mail addresses, and I sent each of them three to five photos, including the two that were currently floating around the Internet.

Then I e-mailed the modeling agencies. While I had been following my photos closely online for the last few weeks, I noticed that a few of them were on modeling agency Web pages. I contacted them directly as well. After I e-mailed the photos, I sat and waited, checking my e-mail and spam box every five seconds to make sure I didn't miss anything.

I didn't have to wait long. In a matter of minutes, I received two replies from half a dozen or so e-mails I sent. Then here came another, then another—and in 24 hours, I had responses from all but one person I reached out to. Everyone was enthused and ready to work with me ASAP!

You would think that the responses I received would confirm that I was, indeed, something special, but I still had my doubts. Besides, what was I supposed to do next? Which one of these people do I work with? Who's the best person to work with? How will I know these people won't try to take advantage of me?

Another thing came to mind that I thought was so funny but very true. If my ass were flat or small, would these people have contacted me back so quickly? If I were a normal female with a normal body, would anybody be as intrigued by me? The answer is HELL, NO! All I could say then was, "Thank God for this ass!" and keep it moving.

Now I had to do my research on the people who responded to my proposal. For the next month or so, I researched all I could to see who and who not to shoot with. I finally decided to shoot with Shawn Dowdell, a photographer from Atlanta. I drove to Atlanta, and we spent a few hours shooting. He had me posing in some awkward, painful positions, but when I saw the photos, it was clear that he knew what he was doing. I was sore as hell the next day, but it was worth it. The pictures were great!

I took those photos and started a Yahoo Group. This was the exact moment I came up with the name "Buffie the Body." Buffie was always an unusual name, and "the Body" was chosen for obvious reasons. So that was it. Buffie the Body was born! The Yahoo Group, as you might have already guessed, took off like a rocket. I had fans signing up to be a part of the Yahoo Group like wildfire. The number of members grew in the thousands in just a week. It took me hours to check my e-mails. People really loved my look.

My next trip was to Houston, Texas, to shoot with Dwyane Darden of *Summerbunnies.com* in the early spring of 2005. I spoke to him a lot on the phone and decided that he was who I wanted to partner with to construct my Web site. I drove 16 hours alone to Houston.

I stayed in Houston for a month. I would shoot with Dwyane during the day and dance in the local clubs at night. When it was time for me to leave Houston, I had made enough money to pay off my Expedition and still had a few thousand left. I had wonderful photos I had taken with Dwyane, and I was very content.

Back home, I continued to build my online presence. I was interacting with my fans, updating my new photos, and constantly checking my e-mail. Among my mass of daily e-mails was a note from Sean Malcolm, an editor at *KING* magazine. What a pleasant surprise! He informed me that they would like to do an interview and use one of my photos for the "Web Girl" column in an upcoming issue.

It wasn't a big section in the magazine, only a quarter page, but I was still thrilled to even be considered for such a huge magazine. I accepted immediately, and he told me he would contact me with more details later.

When *KING* magazine contacted me again, they were requesting that I shoot with their photographer in Miami. They told me that they had been thinking about giving me a seven-page spread in the magazine instead of the quarter page "Web Girl" section that they had previously offered me. I was already in Miami at the time to dance at the local strip clubs there. I had never danced in Miami before, and it was just a coincidence that the shoot was scheduled at the same time.

*KING* e-mailed me a call sheet, and I met the photographer at a hotel alone with his assistant, the makeup artist, the fashion stylist, and a hairstylist. This was my very first official "professional" photo shoot with all the bells and whistles! I didn't have to do my own makeup, I didn't have to bring my own clothes, and I didn't have to do my own hair.

I got to thinking: since these photos were going to be in one of the biggest black men's magazines, was my body really in shape enough to have a seven-page spread? I knew my body was good enough for the strip clubs, and I knew it was good enough for the average nigga, but *KING* was an entirely different ball game. Everyone in the world would see me in this magazine—top-notch modeling agencies, businessmen, white people, casting directors, movie stars, women, kids, trainers—everyone!

I had a few scars on my body from fights when I was growing up, and I had cellulite on the back of my thighs that I developed when I gained weight. I hated the cellulite! I've tried just about every procedure that doctors offered to treat it, and nothing works. I gave up my smooth legs when I opted to gain weight. No one told me I would get cellulite in exchange for a thicker, shapelier figure. If I had to do it all over again, though, I would still say that having cellulite isn't shit compared to the benefits I've enjoyed since I've gained my voluptuous body.

I was unsure and uneasy throughout the entire *KING* photo shoot. I felt like everyone in the room focused on my cellulite and my scars. My hair was already done, so they didn't have to do much with it. Now, the makeup was a little different. I had never in my life had my makeup done professionally. When they started packing all of that makeup on me, I felt insulted. I had great skin, so what's with all the makeup? I've never really cared too much for makeup. I really didn't start wearing makeup until I was in high school. I didn't want to rub anyone the wrong way at the shoot by complaining, so I kept my mouth glued and continued on.

I loved the beautiful swimwear and jewelry that they

dressed me in, but that still didn't take my mind off how disappointed *KING* was going to be when they finally received these photos at their office in New York. I knew they would be pleased with my ass, my stomach, and my face (well, maybe not with all this damned drag queen makeup on!), but the cellulite and the scars may kill my chance of being featured in that seven-page spread.

When the day was over, I was tired as hell and hungry. I try to never eat before or at photo shoots if I can resist. Eating makes my stomach look bloated. One of my best friends, as well as my hairstylist, Perry, had driven to Miami from Atlanta, so when the photo shoot was finished, we went to grab something to eat and went back to our hotel to crash. The next day, we had planned to hit up the strip clubs to see which one I would dance at that night. I knew *KING* should have those photos in their office by now. I guess maybe the scars and the cellulite were too much for their eyes. I'm a very pessimistic person when it comes to waiting on results. I've been like this most of my life. I like to brace for the worst. So, I waited. I continued dancing to make a living.

# Chapter Ten

Tyrone always stayed calm and levelheaded about my success. He never took advantage of me and never asked me for any money. I was traveling a lot as a dancer, so he was used to me being on the road all the time and nothing changed when I started modeling. The house was always clean and intact, the bills were paid, and he was always glad to see me. I had money, I had my health, I had perfect credit, I had my family, I had a supportive boyfriend, I had God, I wasn't dancing anymore, I bought a nice home, and I had two brand-new vehicles in the garage. I was happy, but I was naïve to trust someone and even more naïve to let him stay.

I found out Tyrone was cheating on me. I used his truck one day to take some things to the Goodwill store. I loaded the things on the back of his truck, and I was off.

I'm a very nosy and inquisitive woman when it comes to my men, and you can ask any guy I ever dated in the past. I want to know everything. If they don't tell me, I will find out another way. There won't be any secrets when it comes to me and my man.

I rambled through his truck, leaving no stones unturned. Usually, I come up empty-handed and I'm somewhat satisfied, but not completely. I found a little hole behind the passenger seat. I stuck my hand in and didn't feel anything. I feel like every man cheats, so I just felt like maybe he was one step ahead of me and already disposed of the evidence. When I got to the Goodwill store and had unloaded the truck, I couldn't stop thinking about that hole in the seat. Before leaving the parking lot, I searched that same hole again and BINGO! There was a white plastic sack tied in a knot. I untied the knot and BINGO again! A box of condoms! Let me rephrase that: an *opened* box of condoms!

I was frozen in shock at my discovery. I didn't know what to do. I didn't even cry. I almost felt like I had known all along. I was more relieved that after all these years, I finally caught him, and I knew now that he was a typical man.

He was at work at the time, and I wasn't going to call him there, so I called everyone else. I called Amina, my assistant who I hired after becoming "The Body," and my mother and two sisters, Jennifer and Judy. They thought I was joking at first, but they realized soon enough that I wasn't. They thought I was joking at first, but they realized soon enough that I wasn't. They really liked Tyrone to death and always swore that he could do no wrong.

Tyrone got off work at 7 p.m., so I had 3 hours to hold in my anger until he got there. I laid the bag and the condoms on the counter in the kitchen and left them there until he got home. When he pulled up in driveway, my heart started beating fast. I felt so nauseous that I thought I was going to vomit. I was sitting in the living room when he walked in, talking on his cell phone. He paused briefly and gave me a kiss, then walked past me into the kitchen to put up his lunch bag.

As he walked into the kitchen, I sat on the sofa watching him just to see the expression on his face when he noticed the box of condoms. He noticed it instantly and ended his phone conversation abruptly. By the time he turned around to face me, I had already slapped the fuck out of him and told him to get the fuck out! He grabbed me and fell to his knees, telling me how sorry he was and to please not make him leave. I didn't want to hear it.

"You nasty muthafucker!" I screamed as I started crying. "Get out right now before I kill your fuckin' ass!"

"Please, Buffie," he kept begging and pleading. "I'm sorry. I love you, I don't want to leave." He spoke as if he were crying, but I don't remember seeing any tears. I do remember the hurt and sadness he had on his face as he kept clinging to my legs like a little child.

Finally, when he saw that nothing was working and I wouldn't budge, he got up off the floor, pretending to wipe his eyes, and went to the bedroom to pack. My phone was ringing off the hook because my family and friends knew that Tyrone should have been home by now, so they were calling to see what was going on and to make sure I was okay and I wasn't on my way to jail for voluntary manslaughter. I didn't answer because I wasn't in the mood to talk to anyone.

I stood in the doorway of the bedroom to watch him pack. Slowly but surely he was packing. As he packed, he explained that it was my fault that he was cheating. He went further to say that I never had time for him and I was always gone, and that even when I was home, I was always on the phone or in my office on the computer. He said I lived my life as if he didn't exist.

Believe it or not, every single thing that he said to me was the honest truth. I really couldn't say anything as he rambled on about how he had been neglected and how he didn't feel loved by me anymore. I really felt where he was coming from, but I still made him leave right then out of principle.

I let him come back. Even though he cheated on me, at the end of the day, I still consider him a great person. Call me crazy if you want to. Yea, I know, I'm a punk. He screwed up, but everyone does, and I still loved him.

I continued to travel and host my parties and events across America and Canada. Life continued looking good. Of course, I didn't trust Tyrone at home now. I can say now, after my experiences, that I will never trust any man completely, but that's just how I am. Things continued to get distant between us at home. When things bother me, I'll speak on it. He's the total opposite. He never spoke unless it was necessary. If he was feeling a certain way about something, he never let me know what was on his mind.

I found out through one of my friends in Greensboro, North Carolina, that Tyrone was going to Japan to work for a year. I was driving home from Greensboro at three in the morning. I had just hosted a party at a club called Sugar Bares VIP. My phone rang, and it was my homeboy Bernard calling me from Greensboro, making sure I was safe because he knew I was driving by myself.

"Hello," I answered.

"You good?" Bernard asked.

"I'm a little sleepy, but I'm alright."

We started recapping the night. Earlier, Bernard had shown me how to get to my hotel, because even though I was familiar with Greensboro, I didn't know where my hotel was located. He never came to Sugar Bares that night, so I was telling him how it went. After we discussed what went on in the club, he asked me about Tyrone and whether he had left the country yet.

"What you talking about?" I asked.

"Has Tyrone left to go to Japan yet?"

"Who told you that? Why would you ask that?" I shot back.

"He didn't tell you?"

"Tell me what?"

"That he's going to Japan for a year or so."

"That nigga ain't going nowhere," I said, laughing.

"Okay, but that's what he mentioned to me a few weeks ago, and he seemed serious."

We went back and forth a bit and finally ended the exchange, with me telling Bernard that if Tyrone wanted to go, let him.

I called Tyrone immediately after to ask him about what I had just heard. He halfway confirmed that it was true. He said that he did volunteer to go to Japan, but he didn't know if he was accepted to go yet.

"WHAT! What about *me*? You just going to leave me here in fucking South Carolina by myself, and the only reason I'm here in this boring ass place is because of YOU!" I was screaming at the top of my lungs at three o'clock in the morning on the road. I shouted until I started crying.

"That's so fucked up!" I told him. "You're so motherfuckin' selfish! If you leave, I swear I won't be here when you get back! The house, the dog, and I will be GONE!" I hung up. *Is he serious?! He couldn't be!* I called him right back, but he told me he couldn't talk because he was working and he would call me when he went on break.

*Another person leaving me, and who knows if I will ever see him again.* I couldn't imagine what I would do without him. I didn't know anyone in Spartanburg, where we lived. I didn't have any friends or family in South Carolina.

Months after, it was confirmed that he was leaving. All I could do is think about me being alone and how in the hell I was going to get the fuck out and as far away from South Carolina as possible. All of a sudden, I hated South Carolina *and* him. I went to Atlanta looking for a place to move. I had a lot of trouble finding a place. I didn't want to live around anyone who knew of Buffie the Body because I didn't need the aggravation and headache of everyone knowing where I lived. That was so hard to do in Atlanta since there were so many industry people who lived there. Plus, the traffic is horrible there, and everything is becoming overpriced.

Eventually, I thought of the things that I could do freely in South Carolina that I may not be able to do so freely in Atlanta. If I moved to Atlanta, I would be giving up a lot of the privacy that I cherished in South Carolina. I would give up being able to walk around without people being in my business and taking pictures of me. I do go through that in South Carolina, but not near as much as when I'm in Atlanta. I love to shop in peace, garden in peace, go to the gym in peace, and just live in peace! I really love peace!

I realized why I should like South Carolina enough to stay. It's peaceful as hell! After going back and forth with myself, I decided to stay in South Carolina for a little longer.

I told Tyrone I was going to remain, and I finally came to terms that he had a life, too, and I shouldn't try to hold him back from being what he wants to be in life. He had never tried to hold me back, and I love him for that.

In the last months before he left, I spent more time with him. We even took a vacation to Las Vegas with my family. I was still very sad and would cry when I was alone, but I'm a big girl and the shit I'd been through in my lifetime was much harder than what I was going through now.

When it finally came time for him to go, I was hoping I didn't have to take him to the airport and watch him walk away. I absolutely hate good-byes. I've always found it hard to say good-bye to the people I love. I just don't handle it well at all. I helped him with his luggage, walked him up to the ticket counter, gave him a kiss, and turned and left quickly. I didn't want to witness him crying or have him see me in tears either. I didn't even look back.

While I drove home, I asked God to keep him safe and happy and that's all I wanted. I told myself that if I never saw him again, that's just something I would have to live with. He may have a change of heart, or I may have a change of heart, but whichever happened, I just wanted God to keep him safe. I thought I would never see the day when Tyrone and I would really be apart. But everything happens for a reason. I was trusting in God to carry me to my next phase in life.

I never saw Tyrone again because I eventually felt that

the relationship was truly over and I didn't want to hold him back. I prayed and asked God to keep a close watch on him and send him a good woman that would treat him well and give him the life he deserves. I will always love him. It's hard dealing with some people when you become a celebrity. I lost friends in the beginning because they couldn't deal with me not having much time for them like I used to. But after they realized that I was growing and they were still important to me, my true friends understood and have stayed by my side to this day.

My life hasn't been bad after all. I had to get used to Tyrone not always being around. I really saw after he left how much I depended on him. He was like my backbone, but I had to step it up and learn how to run things on my own. He had taken care of everything in the house for the entire time we lived together. Now everything was on me. I had to learn what days the trash was collected, how to operate the irrigation system for the grass, when to take my vehicles for maintenance, make sure the lawn guy was cutting the grass, make sure the bills were paid on time, and so much more.

There is so much to running a house, but I'm learning quickly. After the first few months, it was like clockwork! I sort of liked having a house to myself and being so independent. It was sort of fun! I learned to manage a household, and I'm very proud of myself. If someone had told me that things would be this easy, I wouldn't have believed it. God showed me the way, and He's been there with me every step.

See, all my life I've always had a boyfriend. I was always either jumping into the next relationship as soon as I was out of one, or I was already in the next one when the last one ended. I guess this is like my downtime. I like being in a relationship, but I like to be in a *healthy* relationship. People always want to know what type of guy strikes Buffie's attention. I like a good variety of men, as you can tell from what I've told you. I've had good guys and not-so-good guys.

I dated a man back when I was living in Athens in 1999 that was very abusive. I had never had a black eye until I met him. I never thought I could even have a black eye because I was dark-skinned! He proved me wrong on that. He had been to jail more times than I can count, and I knew this before I started dating him, but I let him spend the night at my house one night. We had sex, and it was on after that. Seems like after that night, we started dating and he never left.

We dated for about a year or so off and on. We fought all the time. He vandalized my truck, threatened to kill my family, and would come and ring my doorbell all night. When I didn't open the door, he would rip my doorbell out and take it with him. I would call the police on him and have him locked up, but I would be the fool and take him back every time.

The last straw happened one morning when I drove him

to work.  He was upset because I told him he wouldn't see me anymore after that day.  He went crazy.  When we arrived at his job, he went to get out and slapped the fuck out of me. I started screaming, and when I tried to jump out of the truck, he grabbed me and tore my pants.  I fell out of the truck onto the parking lot, and he jumped into the driver's seat and drove off, leaving me lying in the parking lot.  The police came, I pressed charges, and that was it with us.  He was charged with aggravated stalking on some pervious events, battery, and theft of my truck, and was locked up.

I don't know what in the fuck possessed me to stay as long as I did with him.  The only good thing about our entire relationship was that he was mind-blowing in bed.  Getting locked up seemed to be the only thing that would finally keep him away from me.

I stepped outside the box last year and started dating a man with kids.  His name was Adrian.  He was a very handsome, 36, tall, dark-skinned with a low haircut, and he was in law enforcement.  He had a slim sort of build, but he was muscular because he went to the gym every single day. Come to find out, everything he had told me about himself in the beginning was a damn lie.

Instead of having a *couple* of kids, he had *five*.  Throw in three baby mamas, no home, and a roommate.  Ladies, can you imagine?  What a damn fool.  After I figured him out, I came to learn that child support was eating him alive. He never had money.  On top of that, two of the three baby

baby mamas were always calling his phone about bullshit that most of the time didn't even pertain to the kids. I cared about the dude, and we did have some good times together, but the fact that he had all these kids, no money, and no real business constantly bothered me and added fuel to the fire. And he was always accusing me of cheating, when I absolutely never did.

Everything about his 36-year-old ass was a big NO-NO. Can you spell D-I-S-A-S-T-E-R? That relationship didn't even get off the ground well. I really liked the man, but he had too many obligations and responsibilities for me, so I told him to leave one day after fussing with him and told him to never call me again. I missed him, but I had to let him go.

I love men who have positive outlooks on life and have goals and ambitions. You don't have to be rich, but you do have to have a job. I suppose as I got deeper into the industry, it became more difficult to find a stable relationship with industry men or civilian niggas. After Tyrone left and I learned the household caretaker game, Buffie the Body kept on keepin' on.

# Chapter Eleven

Pinch me and tell me if I'm dreaming! Don't wake me up if I am dreaming! Say *what*!? G-Unit's Tony Yayo wants me to be in his first music video!? I need to call the G-Unit office ASAP!

"What-the-fuck-ever" is exactly what I said to myself when I read that e-mail from some man claiming to work for G-Unit. Boy, boy, boy, the lies niggas tell to try to get with me. I ignored that e-mail and went to the next one. The next day, I saw the same e-mail address in my inbox. Again, he's telling me that Tony Yayo wants me in his video and G-Unit wants to speak with me, please. He left a phone number. *This guy is really trying to get at me*, I thought. *Does he really think I'm that young and stupid enough to believe this?* Once again, I didn't reply.

A few days later, another e-mail from him came to

my inbox. I decided to call the New York number, but I pressed *67 so my number wouldn't be revealed to whoever answered.

"G-Unit!" someone said when they picked up. I hung up immediately. Now, how could that creep know it was me? *He couldn't! There was no way of him knowing it was me. Maybe this really was G-Unit ... maybe.* Right away I called Sean Malcolm, an editor for *KING* magazine, and told him what was going on and asked him if he could call the same number and confirm that it was, indeed, G-Unit's office, since the *KING* magazine office was in New York as well.

Sean agreed to call them and said he would call me back. Half an hour later, he called and said that it was G-Unit, and yes, they really did want me to be in Tony Yayo's video. I almost died! I couldn't stop yelling and screaming!

"Oh my god! Are you serious?" I shouted.

Sean told me to give them a call, and I did. I was nervous as shit! Initially, I spoke with a guy named Jay Johnson. He explained what was going on. He said that he and Clap, who had been sending me the e-mails, had seen my photos Online, and they showed them to Yayo. Yayo was floored and said that I had to be in his video. I left my number for them to give me a call when Yayo and 50 Cent were in the office.

Yayo called me later. I was so nervous I couldn't talk. He told me how he wanted me as the main girl in his video.

but he had just one question.

"What?" I asked.

"Is it real?"

"Is what real?" I asked.

"Your ass?"

Of all the things that would qualify a person for a job! I yelled, "Hell, yes!"

When I received the e-mails from G-Unit, I was hesitant to respond. I was sure that this was just some nigga tryin' to get in my jeans. The things men have done to get my attention in recent years! The list could go on for miles.

When I did finally talk to Tony Yayo, I felt like it was all a dream. 50 Cent even got on the phone to say hello. He told me about Yayo and the video. Once I got off the phone with them, I couldn't hold my tongue. I started calling everyone I knew, telling them who I had just spoken with. My family and friends were shocked.

For the next few weeks, Yayo kept in contact with me almost every day. He spoke with my mother and my sister. We would chat all day long, just getting to know each other. I was still dancing, doing my thing from city to city. One day, while I was in Miami shooting for *KING*, I got a phone call that afternoon after the shoot from Yayo. He was requesting that I get on the next plane to NYC for the music video shoot.

I was like, "*What!?*" What was I supposed to do with my truck, which I had driven to Miami, and what would I do with Perry, my hairstylist, who accompanied me? I asked Perry if he would like to go to New York with me for the shoot, and he was all for it. We immediately packed up, checked out of the hotel in Miami, and drove nonstop (except for gas) back to Atlanta. I drove all night long while Perry slept. We made it back to his place outside of Atlanta the next morning. He did my hair so I would be prepared for the shoot. The next day, we jumped on a flight and headed to the Big Apple!

We arrived in New York and were greeted by Perry's cousin, Renee, who lived in the city. That night, we stayed at Renee's place. I had bubble guts like crazy all day. Here I was in a big city (I had only been to New York one time prior), shooting my first music video and meeting G-Unit. All of this was just too much for a little country girl from Athens, Georgia.

The music director had informed me that even though I was the main girl, they didn't need me there for the entire 2-day shoot. I was only scheduled for the second day. I hung out the first day and did some window-shopping.

That evening, I received a call from one of the producers of the video shoot. She told me they had changed the itinerary, and they needed me to come in to check my hair and do a wardrobe check. It sounded sort of fishy to me, because she didn't sound too sure if she really needed me there or not. It almost seemed as if someone were standing next to her, coaching her on what to tell me. I told her it was no problem and that she could send a car to scoop me up if they needed me. A van arrived an hour or so later, and I was off to the shoot with butterflies like crazy. I was finally going to meet G-Unit face to face. I wasn't ready for this at all!

The shoot was in Long Island. It was cold as hell outside that night. The location was an amazing building that was decorated like a luxurious mansion, but I think they said it was a culinary school of some sort.

When I arrived, they took me directly into a small trailer where hair and makeup was. I sat down in the chair so the hairstylist could go over my hairstyles for the shoot the next day. The trailer was crowded, and it got even more packed when people found out I had made it there. Everyone wanted to come and take a look at what's been the most talked about ass of the video world yet. I didn't say anything. I just watched how people kept making excuses to come in and get an eyeful. I still didn't see the point of me being there a day early, because even if I got my hair done that night, they still would have to redo it tomorrow. After the hairstylist played in my hair for 45 minutes, I went over to the wardrobe trailer so I could try on some clothes.

The wardrobe trailer was a little calmer. But not for long! Seems like one person would come in to get a peek at me, and that person would leave and go and tell someone else, and then they would come and so on and so on. I think that happened all night. It was like they had never seen a female shaped like me before. The stylist, Misa Hylton-Brim, also known as Sean Combs' baby mama, gave me a few dresses to go into the bathroom to try on.

I took the dresses and went into the bathroom. As I tried on each dress, I would come out to show her how it fit. After trying on four or five dresses, I was done. As I changed back into my own clothes in the bathroom, I heard the front trailer door open again. Another Curious George.

I came out of the bathroom and immediately walked right into 50 Cent. I thought I had swallowed my tongue, and my heart stopped for 5 seconds. He caught me with my mouth open like I had seen a ghost. I was flabbergasted and embarrassed at the same time. He shook my hand and introduced himself in a very polite and gentle way, with a slightly boyish smile, as if he were just as surprised to see me. He was such a nice person with a clean, innocent demeanor. Standing directly behind him was my boy Yayo, the man I've been talking to on the phone for weeks! He gave me a big hug and said hello. Now Yayo had bit of cockiness about him, but I already knew this about his personality from our long conversations, so I was happy to match a voice to a real man. He was still a gentleman.

We all sat down and started chatting. The rest of the crew came in, and I was introduced to everyone. They had all been on set earlier when I had initially arrived. They had finally made their way to me so they could inspect the girl that they had chosen to be the featured female in their video. I could tell by the whispers, nods, and facial expressions that I wasn't a disappointment. Matter of fact, I was told that I looked even better in person. Boy, I was relieved that I passed inspection!

After talking with 50 Cent for a while, he revealed to me that he was the reason that I was called to come in earlier than originally planned. He told me that he had to see me in person to confirm that I was really built like I was in my photos. He explained to me how he wouldn't be on set at all tomorrow because he was shooting a movie in Canada, and he wanted to meet me before he left.

I knew it! I knew they didn't really need me here for hair. The woman that phoned me was just too ashamed to tell me the real reason why they needed me here at the shoot all of a sudden. I wasn't mad at 50 at all. Shit, if I'm paying top dollar for a female to be featured in one of the G-Unit videos, then I'd need to see if she really looks like she does in her pictures. Everyone knows in this industry that airbrushing and Photoshop is a girl's best, best friend! I'm glad I passed the inspection!

The shoot went very well. There were other video girls there, but you would have never known!

"Buffie, are you okay? Do you need anything?"

"Are you hungry, Buffie?"

"Get Buffie into hair and makeup, please!"

"Where's Buffie?!"

I really felt like royalty. Everyone was so attentive to my needs. I will always appreciate the fact that my first video shoot was so professional and so well-planned. I didn't have a single problem at all. Even the other girls didn't seem to mind how they were completely pushed to the side and ignored. I know it was obvious to them that I was the important female that day. The video went well into the wee hours of the frigid morning. I was absolutely exhausted by the time the shoot wrapped up. I took photos with everyone, said my good-byes, and I was off, back to reality.

It took forever, it felt like, for that video to finally come on TV. I hadn't talked much about it to the other girls in the strip clubs because I didn't want them to laugh at me if the whole thing was a flop. When it did air, though, I went foolish! I was texting and calling *everyone*. My phone wouldn't stop ringing. I couldn't believe I was on TV! I felt like a diamond in the rough and that the world had been sleeping on me. A dark-skinned, thick chick in a G-Unit video, and I was the main girl up close and so personal!

I finally got a call back from *KING* magazine, and I was dead wrong about the feeling I had had during the shoot. They loved all of the photos. They said they were everything they had hoped for, and I was granted my seven pages. A major music video and a seven-page spread all within months of being in the industry. I got paid for the video a few weeks later, but I was told that I would not get paid for the magazine spread. The editor said that they never pay the girls to shoot for them. Well, damn, you would think that the females would get paid to appear in *KING*. I didn't believe him, but after I asked around to see if I should ask for at least a little something for the shoot, I was given an all-around "No!" Oh well, who cares? I was still going to have a spread in the magazine, and that was good enough for me.

My Web site officially launched April 15th, and the *KING* magazine spread hit the stands right after. I didn't know which way to turn! My life was so different now. No one will ever understand how all of this made me feel. How did I get so lucky all of a sudden? Where did all of this come from? I asked the Lord to stay by my side and help me make the right decisions, because everybody was coming at me so swiftly that I could hardly keep up.

I noticed that after I had done all of this, I hadn't made any money outside of what I was paid for the Tony Yayo video; that was it. *Damn, am I going to be famous but broke? I thought this would be my sure way out of the strip clubs. Lord, I'm so ready to get out of the strip game!* The clubs had been good to me, and I can't deny that, but it's time to make a change, and I just knew this would be my foot out the door.

God was listening to my prayer. My first week's check

from my Web site was $2,400. For *1 week*! The second week's check was $2,700. For *1 week*! You're telling me that all I have to do is put sexy, nonnude swimsuit photos on my Web site and charge people $19.99 to look at them? *That's it?* God had really answered my prayer! My strip club days were over! I never danced in another strip club again.

The month after the G-Unit video came out, I went on to shoot for *XXL* Eye Candy of the Month and I shot the cover of *BlackMen* magazine. This was the first magazine to place me on their cover. They gave me another cover called the SSX Edition. When a model gets an SSX Edition, the entire magazine is dedicated just to her. No other model appeared in that magazine but me! I ended up with about five SSX Edition magazines, all dedicated to me. After *BlackMen* came *Smooth* magazine. I was also on the cover of the *Smooth*, and the shoot was in gorgeous Jamaica.

My life changed virtually overnight, and I was working constantly on photo shoots, video shoots, my Web site, calendar shoots, and social and professional appearances. I hired a team of professionals to help keep me from going crazy. The e-mails I started receiving, let alone scheduling and planning my trips and events, were enough to make my head spin.

I went from dancing for celebrities to taking press photos with them at industry events and social gatherings. Almost every member of the sports and entertainment industry I've

The photo that started the Buffie the Body craze! Taken in Baltimore, 2004.

My brother, Charles Hardy, and myself.

Skinny as hell! 119 lbs in 19

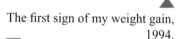

The first sign of my weight gain, 1994.

Lamont and me at his high school prom in 1990.

My sister, Atline Hardy, at her prom.

Me, Eric Parker and Amina
Diop in New York, 2007.

50 Cent, Tony Yay
and me at the "So
Seductive" shoot,
NYC 2005.

T-Pain and me
in Charlotte,
2006.

8 Ball and
MJG in
Memphis,
2007.

PHOTO SIL

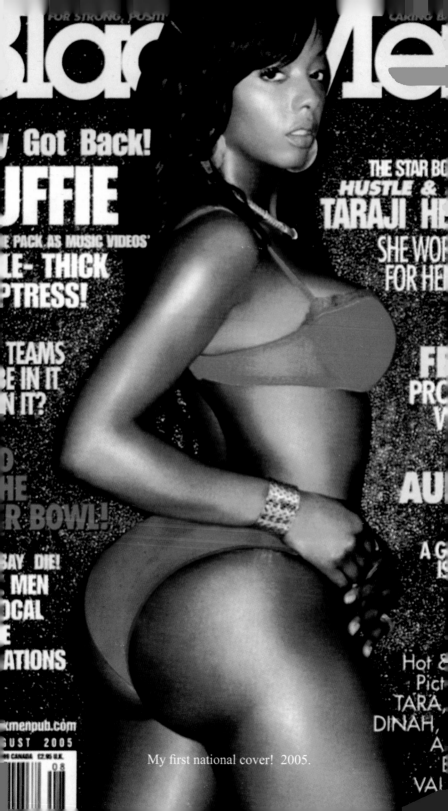

Blac Men

FOR STRONG, POSIT

CARING B

y Got Back!

UFFIE

E PACK AS MUSIC VIDEOS'

LE- THICK

PTRESS!

TEAMS
BE IN IT
N IT?

D
HE
R BOWL!

BAY DIE!
MEN
OCAL
E
ATIONS

xmenpub.com

GUST 2005

CANADA £2.95 U.K.

08

THE STAR BO
HUSTLE & J
TARAJI HE
SHE WOF
FOR HEI

FE
PRO
V

AU

A G
IS

Hot &
Pict
TARA
DINAH,
A

VAL

My first national cover! 2005.

Yung Joc and me
Memphis, 2007.

Tigger and me
playing around i
Phoenix, 2006.

*BlackMen*
Swimsuit Issue, 2

Juelz Santana and
me in Miami 2006.

Allen Iverson with
me in Philly, 2005.

Me and Shaq in Miami on the set of "You Can't Stop the Reign," 2006.

Common and me at a signin at George's Music Room, Chicago 2007

Irv Gotti and me in Philly, 2006.

Me, Vivca and Morris Chestnut in Detroit, 2006.

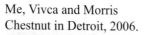

Me and Luke Campbell at a Superbowl party in Detroit, 2006.

legwork photography

Me and Too Short hangin out in Oakland, 2006.

Mike Jones and me at Club Ice Age in Houston, 2006.

*BlackMen* Lingerie Issue, 2007.

Young Jeezy and m
in Richmond, 2006

Tracy McGrady an
me in Houston, 200

Me, Bun B and
Latoya Luckett in
Houston 2005.

either done business with or met on a personal or social level has been just as excited to meet me as I was to meet them.

In 2007, for instance, I was walking through the Charlotte Douglas Airport when someone grabbed my arm. He stopped me because I didn't even notice him. I can't believe I missed all that sexiness! Tyrese gave me a big hug and asked if I ever go to Los Angeles. We exchanged e-mail addresses, and he rushed off to his gate. I was smiling like a fool for the next hour. Now that is a fine, thick, sexy muthafucker! We've stayed in touch since then through text messaging.

I was at an event during the Kentucky Derby when I ran into Jermaine Dupree. We were in the same VIP section together. He wasn't arrogant but very friendly. He's extremely short, but I think most people know this. One of the photographers wanted us to get a picture together, and he was very willing to do so.

Outside of urban models, everyone in the industry have been nothing other than downright kind and very respectful. After all, we all came from somewhere; most of us weren't privileged children, and a good number of us have lived through very tough times, just like everyone else. I just won the lottery, that's all—and my ass was the winning ticket.

# Chapter Twelve

Something strange started happening after I stopped dancing. I started having dreams. Erotic dreams. Dreams about being with women in a sexual way. The strange thing is that I never had these dreams when I was a stripper. What was wrong with me?

Easily two times a week for almost a year I would dream about screwing females. My dreams would be about me grinding on women, licking them on their chests, or receiving oral pleasure from a woman. That shit was off the chain! I swear on everything I love in this world, it felt so good, a true story!

I would wake up and find myself grinding on the mattress or the sheets on the bed. Yes, it was *that* serious! There were times where I was enjoying my dream so much that I was disappointed if I woke up too soon. I would wake up and just lie in the bed and wonder what in the fuck was wrong with me. I wanted to know so badly why I was having such crazy dreams. Was it because I wanted to try it? Was it that a pack of females was going to rape me soon and take my cookies? Shit, I wish I knew the answers.

I've never actually been with a woman, but there were girls who hit on me all the time while I was working in the clubs. It's much more flattering to get hit on by a woman than a man, in my opinion. Men are just that—MEN! It doesn't take much to tempt the eye of a man, but a woman's eye is a little more observant of their prey. Women are more vocal, persistent, and sensitive than most men.

I've had a few dancers in the club rub and grind on me. I would stop them immediately because if I didn't, I knew I might let them continue. Yes, a few times I almost fell for a female's advances.

One night, I was dancing in Atlanta. I was on stage with a girl named Sho Nuff. We were twisting next to each other, when suddenly she grabbed me and started grinding. She was fine and built just like me, but I was not about to get turned out by a dancer. I pushed her off in a joking way and ran to the dressing room. She came in later and apologized. We laughed it off, but really I didn't think it was funny.

The main reason I held back is the thought that I may have to eat pussy. I can't emphasize this enough: I love getting head. I love, love, *love* it! While I overindulge in receiving oral sex from men, I don't know how long I could get away with always being the receiver in a lesbian relationship. I would always want it, but would never want to give it in return. And that would probably be a problem in any of my potential gay relationships. I know too much about pussies from working near them for so long. I've seen more pussies up close than an OBGYN. I don't think I could easily just put someone's peach in my mouth and enjoy it. I did hear that women give head better than men. If I let a woman eat my pussy, then it may be over for me ever dating a man again.

Over the years, I've found some dancers to be extremely sexy to me. I would never approach them on a sexual level. I would only admire from afar and leave it alone. It seems like it's so popular for women to be gay these days. It's not looked at as being negative. It's like it's the "in thing" now. I don't have a problem with seeing two women together, but I have a problem with seeing two men together.

What had taken place in my dreams I would never have the guts to try in real life. If I do it with a woman, then does that make me "officially" gay? Even if I did it just one time, would I be considered gay? How on earth would I tell my family that I'm a lesbian and I'm licking crotches now? To be honest, I'd do it the same way I told them I was a stripper. Just tell them and let them deal with their own emotions. They never know what to expect from me. My brothers and sisters are married, average, everyday working, family-oriented people, and nothing more, nothing less. I

I don't know what in hell went wrong with me and my brother Charles. We certainly took alternate paths in life. I was fighting, dating drug dealers, stealing, stripping, and selling pussy ... I've done it all. Luckily, my wild life didn't hold me back from being successful as I am now. I'm sure being a lesbian wouldn't hurt anything either!

# Chapter Thirteen

I did two more videos after the Tony Yayo video, "Oh Yes," by Juelz Santana, and the 2006 remix of "You Can't Stop the Reign," by DJ Kayslay, DJ Greg Street, Papoose, Bun B, and Shaq. I was late to the Juelz video because I had been shooting for a magazine, so they just fit me in and didn't give me the main role.

The Juelz shoot was in Los Angeles. It was the day after the Vibe Awards, in mid-November 2005, for which I was nominated Vibe Vixen of the Year. I really wasn't interested in doing another music video, but since I was already in LA doing a photo shoot for *BlackMen* magazine, I said, what the heck.

I shot all morning, all day, and half the night with *BlackMen* magazine. We started at 9 a.m. and didn't finish until 10 p.m. that night. When I finally finished with the photo shoot, I was rushed off to the Juelz video shoot about an hour and a half away. The fashion editor of *BlackMen* had agreed to drive me to the shoot, but we got lost, and it took us forever to find the spot. When we finally got there, the shoot was just about over. There were other models there, but for the most part, most of the people had left.

The staff took me into a trailer that had "Makeup and Hair" written on the door. I went inside, and there were two other models getting their faces and hair done. I sat down on the sofa and waited until the other models were finished, and then they started on me. My hair and makeup were basically already done because I had just left a shoot. They just touched me up and sent me over to wardrobe to find something to wear.

Just as I had predicted, they didn't have anything in wardrobe that would fit me or that I thought was appropriate. I ended up wearing some jeans that I had worn to the shoot and a pink and white T-shirt that I hated.

When I was finished with wardrobe, the staff rushed me down the hill where I finally met Juelz. He smiled and gave me a big hug and told me a little about the shoot. Because I got there so late and 90 percent of the video had been already been shot, my part was so tiny I almost felt like it wasn't even worth it. I went ahead and did it anyway though. It took maybe an hour and six retakes, and we were finished. Juelz was a really nice man. He looked really young, and he was much shorter than I am, but I thought he was cute. We exchanged numbers, and I left.

The "You Can't Stop the Reign" shoot was in Miami. Bun B was there, Shaq, Papoose, Remy, Greg Street, and Kayslay. I've never met anyone larger than Shaq. He towered over everyone. He was a nice guy, very funny and full of energy. Since the shoot, I've spent some time with him at social gatherings.

The shoot seemed unorganized initially, but eventually, everything started falling into place. The shoot was in a club on South Beach during the day. There was a ton of girls on the set. I didn't know any of them, but you better know that anywhere you see rappers and ball players, there are going to be chicks—and a lot of them at that.

Video shoots normally last anywhere from 8 to 12 hours, but I was only at this one for a few hours. I had a calendar signing in Baltimore that same night, so I couldn't stay long. I went inside the restroom to do my hair and makeup. They had a makeup artist and hairstylist there, but I didn't like the way the other girls' hair or makeup was looking. It didn't look professional at all to me. I felt like I could do a much better job on myself, and I did. I brought my own outfit to the shoot, because I couldn't trust that someone would have anything to fit me that I actually liked.

After I was dressed, Kayslay suggested to the director to

go ahead and shoot all my scenes at once so I could get to the airport. It took about 3 hours to finish my scenes. After the director was satisfied with what he had shot, they gave me permission to go. Kayslay had a car service take me back to the airport.

I did those three videos and was never interested in doing any more. Of course, there are rumors that I have sex with people to get in magazines and videos, but they were born from people, mostly other models, who don't know me or know how I play the game. People thought I slept with Tony Yayo, and they asked if I ever slept with 50 Cent. My answer has and always will be "no." I never had sex with either of those men, and never even came close. I think 50 Cent is fine as hell, but I never wanted to sleep with him. I was in love with his hustle and his drive.

There were only a few times that I went outside my regular groove and dated someone in the sports and entertainment industry. I've often been asked by my fans and my industry friends what attracted me to Kayslay and Gucci Mane. My answer has always been the same. There is something special about a person on the inside that most people, not even close friends or family, can see. It's usually something that a woman feels and understands about a man, and it is almost impossible to put into words. Something exists between two people that doesn't manifest in other daily interactions. I'm not a female to always be hung up on how a dude looks as much as how he treats me and makes me feel.

I liked the way Kayslay treated me when I first met him. We didn't start dating until after I hosted a party for him. He booked me and flew me to New York to host his birthday party in 2005. In the beginning, Keith wasn't pressed about trying to be with me like most guys who meet me are. I knew he found me attractive, and I'm sure he wanted to have sex with me, but he concealed it well. He was very smooth, respectable, and business-minded.

He met me in the lobby of my hotel before the party. He paid my hosting fee, made sure I was okay during the event, got me back to the hotel safe, and didn't call me anymore that night or the next day. He didn't try to come to my room after the party, didn't try to run any game, didn't try to take me to breakfast (most men have a way of trying to take me home afterwards), and wasn't blowing my phone up.

I was really surprised. Nine out of ten parties don't end like that. You get promoters and all types of industry niggas blowing your phone up all night and the next day, trying to take you shopping, to dinner, to the movies, or just trying to hang out. Keith did none of this—and that, along with his unbelievable swagger—had my mind going crazy, wanting to know more about him.

Keith always took me to the nicest restaurants in New York City, and we had a great time together. He loves seafood as much as I do, so we would go to his favorite spot, The Crab House, and we frequented Mr. Chow. When he was out on business, I would go shopping with his driver and meet him back at his spot later. He had a lot of fans, and a lot of men who were trying to get into the rap game looked up to him and would stop us a lot. We never went many places outside of restaurants, because we both love to eat. Most of the time, we would just chill at his place.

Of all the things people said to me about him ("he's mean," "he's rough," "he hangs out in strip clubs with strippers all the time," "he has a quick temper and is always starting drama"), none of it seemed to be true when I was with him. If he did hang out with strippers, then at least he didn't bring the strip club home. I had never seen him in any photos with any females, and I've never known him to be linked to any notorious women when I met him. He has one of the nicest hearts I know; he's incredibly caring and helps people out.

Still, after dating him for a time, our personalities starting clashing like hell. He's a true New Yorker at heart, and I'm a true Down South chick to the bone. Our way of thinking and our views on life and relationships ultimately did us in. We were separated more than we were together. It became obvious that we probably wouldn't make it as a couple. We're still cool, and there are no hard feelings between us. Today, we get along better as friends than lovers.

On the other hand, Gucci was country and Southern as hell, just like me. I felt I could relate to him more because he reminded me of the type of guys that I was accustomed to dating. I met Radric in 2006 in Atlanta at the Clubhouse

Restaurant in the Lenox Square Mall. He hadn't been out of jail that long before I met him. His demeanor was thuggish, street nigga, drug dealer, hustler, and he don't give a fuck about going to jail. He's just a plain hood nigga! Yea, yea— I always fall for those types of niggas. But he was so damn cute. I loved his long eyelashes and black wavy hair.

When Radric and I were traveling together, we would always get two hotel rooms because I don't like anyone around me smoking weed. He had to have his weed, so we would use one room for him to smoke in and the other room we would sleep in. All of this was just too much for me. He wasn't a hard person to deal with; I just needed him to be a little more mindful of his actions and be more mature about certain situations. Most of the time we hung out in Atlanta, but we would often meet up in passing when we would be hosting parties. We often planned to take a vacation together, but it never happened because we were both so busy at the time.

What I think went wrong with us is that I'm older than Gucci, so his way of life and my way of life are entirely different. When I was his age, I was into the same type of things that he's into now. The loud music (we often fussed about it when we were in his car), hanging in the hood, hanging with his homeboys, hanging in clubs every weekend, and just being wild and uninhibited became too much for me.

When people are young, there's nothing wrong with that

type of lifestyle, but the fast life was behind me, and I was not trying to go back and relive it just to be with him. I'm a very mellow person now. I don't hang out, I don't run with a group of females, I don't drink, I don't smoke, and I like to chill at home when I'm not out making moves and making money.

I eventually decided that I had to walk away from the relationship before his lifestyle starting affecting me and my life negatively. I stopped answering my phone when he called and eventually changed my number.

Almost a year later, while I was in LA taping a pilot for a reality show, a publicist walked up to me and said, "So *you're* the infamous Buffie the Body. You just made front page news!" and then he showed me his Blackberry. On his screen read, "Buffie the Body Pregnant!" I almost collapsed. I read further to discover that I was pregnant by Gucci Mane. I almost lost my mind. Next thing you know, people were calling me from Baltimore, Atlanta, Ohio, New York, Philly, and California, all wanting to know if it was true. The shit was all over the radio morning shows and all over the message boards.

First of all, when this news broke, I hadn't seen Gucci in 8 months. I had completely cut ties, changed my number, and moved on. So how could I be pregnant by a dude I haven't seen in almost a year? Then people started telling me that Gucci was not happy about it either. I had my assistant contact him and his team to try to get to the bottom of this. In the meanwhile, I had my team contact all of the message boards and have them remove the rumor at once. My assistant informed me that Gucci's manager thought we had something to do with putting the rumor out. That was just icing on the cake. Why in the fuck would I do something like that? What can I gain by telling people I'm pregnant by Gucci Mane? That shit was so stupid to me.

If anything, it would hurt my career tremendously. My success rides on my physical appearance. I would never try to further my career by getting pregnant and potentially losing what made me famous—my body. I'm not a lazy chick, and I'm not one of these dependent ass females who sleep around with celebrities just to get pregnant and get a check every month. I have my own life, and I want my own money. Not only that, but being romantically linked to Radric didn't, and will never, help me in my career.

I wanted to tell Gucci's people that they were shallow and really feeling themselves if they even halfway believed that hoe-ass shit! But you know what? I left the shit alone and kept it moving. I've never spoken on this subject publicly until now. I didn't want to keep it going, so I just kept doing what I do and prayed that the drama would go away. At the end of the day, I'm not mad at Gucci about anything. I was a little disappointed that he would believe that I would start a rumor, and he knows what type of female I am. I never told anyone about me dating him because it was never anyone's business. I think his folks put that shit in his head, but at the end of the day, it is what it is.

I've never been a "Superhead" type of female. I've never had a bad name or was ever tied up in a scandal. I always desired more in a relationship than just sex, and I have no need to use my body to get into shoots and create industry connections. I love attention, quality time, and honesty, and it's hard enough getting it all from a man, let alone an industry nigga!

# Chapter Fourteen

My relationship with Chad Johnson of the Cincinnati Bengals was really a fling. I didn't try to force a more serious connection; not because I wasn't attracted to him, but because I knew it would be too challenging and stressful trying to be with him on a higher level than casual dating. I don't know how the message boards got wind of me dealing with Chad because we were never a very official couple. I really liked him, and he was a very nice person—not at all arrogant like he is on the football field. I'm not into dating athletes like most models are, but Chad just caught me off-guard.

I met him my first year in the industry. He reached out to me through a promoter I knew in Cincinnati. When the promoter told me he was a professional football player, it didn't make me any more willing to give out my number. The promoter called me a few more times, and I eventually agreed to give him my number to pass to Chad. Chad called, and we spoke on the phone for a month or so. I finally agreed to fly to Cincinnati and hang out with him. I only saw Chad in Cincinnati. Since it was football season, he wasn't able to leave. Cincinnati was a little boring to me, and on top of that, it was cold as hell, and I hate cold temperatures. Regardless of the city's conditions, Chad was a very respectable man and was fun to hang out with. He was a funny person and always had me laughing. We enjoyed the time we spent together, and that was good enough for me. I never had any beef with him, because it wasn't that type of relationship. We just rolled with the flow and didn't worry about anything else, and we still keep in touch.

The first time I met Chad, he had a car service pick me up from the airport because he was at football practice. After practice, he met me at this famous soul food restaurant where I was hanging out getting my eat on. I was standing in the parking lot of the restaurant, chatting with some fans, when he pulled up in a purple Hummer. He jumped out and gave me a big hug.

"So we finally meet," I said, and we both laughed. He chatted with the people who were standing out front, and then we got into the Hummer and left. He was such a cool person. He was silly and likes to laugh and act silly, which I loved about him. We drove around Cincinnati for a while as Chad pointed out some sights. He eventually took me to my room and told me he would be back after I got dressed so we could go out that night.

He came back about 2 hours later. He met me in the lobby of the hotel, and we took off. We went out to this nice steakhouse that was downtown. People love Chad in Cincinnati. They treat him like Elvis, especially white people. His fans would not leave him alone. All night, he was signing autographs. I didn't mind at all. I thought it was cool how white people embraced him. After dinner, we just drove around and talked most of the night, because there is nothing to really do in Cincinnati if you don't want to drink.

The next day, he had to go to practice. He made me an appointment to go to the spa for an all-day glamour fest. I had never been to a day spa in my life, so it was definitely a new experience for me.

He picked me up after my day of beauty ended, and we went to grab something to eat at a P.F. Chang's. That was the first time I had ever eaten there, but since that night, it has become one of my all-time favorite restaurants. I think I've been to every single one in the United States now.

The next morning, he took me to the airport, and I gave him a hug and kiss and thanked him for a wonderful time. I had good thoughts about him when I left. Any dude, especially an industry player, that can show me a good time and not expect sex on the first date is always a winner to me. I really couldn't believe he never said anything to me about trying to fuck. I really liked him. Maybe I was wrong. Maybe all niggas aren't the same.

I visited Chad again about a month later. He flew me to Cincinnati once more. The date didn't go any differently. We did a little shopping at the local malls, we ate, and that's about it. The second time, I stayed at his house. He had a nice condo that was very clean and well decorated. We watched movies on television that evening, and we eventually fell asleep.

The next day, he had a game. I think they were playing the Steelers. I hated football and had no intentions of going to the game. Besides, it was cold as hell that day and drizzling rain. He tried to convince me to come to the game, but I wouldn't go. He left me in bed and told me if I decided to come I could ride with his brothers. After he left, I got up, cleaned up his room, and made my way to the airport to go home. I called his phone and left a message and told him I would call him when I made it back.

The third time we hung out, we slept together for the first time. And what should have been an amazing trip turned out to be one of the most tragic events in my life.

I will never forget that day. I had just spoken with my sister the day before. I had arrived in Cincinnati to hang out with Chad. He had flown my current hairstylist, Javon, up from Atlanta to do my hair for the weekend. Javon and I arrived at the Millennium Hotel around 5 p.m. Friday in a black Towncar that Chad had waiting for us when we landed at the airport. As we entered the hotel, my phone rang. I searched through my huge, deep purse to finally answer the phone on the last ring.

"Hello," I said.

"What you doing?" Atline asked me in a happy, perky voice.

"Just getting off the plane and just made it to the hotel, why?" I said.

"I just wanted to know, are you coming home to see me for Thanksgiving?"

"I don't know, Atline. All depends on how I'm feeling."

"Please!" she yelled.

I took a deep breath and exhaled. "Yea, I'll be by there."

"Buffie said she's coming to see me!" I heard her holler at my mother with incredible excitement in her voice.

"OK, Atline, I got to go so Javon can start on my hair."

"OK, bye!" she said quickly and hung up.

That was the last time I ever spoke to her.

Chad and I made love that night. The next afternoon, we went to the mall together. It was a sunny day, but still cold as hell. We did a little shopping and strolled around the mall. Every 5 minutes, someone was stopping him or me for an autograph or a picture.

I got a call from my brother, Andre, around 3 o'clock, telling me that Atline was rushed to the hospital. My heart sunk low in my chest. He told me he would call me back and let me know what was going on. I was looking at a pair of shoes when Andre called me back, about an hour later. I think Chad had gone into the Apple store to browse. I *knew* it wasn't good news.

When I answered, he told me Atline was gone. I slammed the shoe in my hand on the display table, held my head down, and started crying. I was trying my best to keep it together because I didn't want people walking up to me, asking me what was wrong or if I was alright, but I just couldn't hold it in.

I walked out of the store, wiping my eyes, not knowing which way to walk, towards Chad or away from him. He was heading in my direction, and he could tell something was very wrong. When he finally got to me, I told him my sister had just passed.

His eyes instantly went soft. He held me close and kept saying how sorry he was. I told him I had to get home, but that I couldn't get on a plane. I wanted to drive home. I was too emotional to be around people or to be cramped up on an airplane. I wanted to be by myself, and I knew that 8-hour drive would be relaxing and comforting for me. We left the mall and went back to his place. He gave me the keys to his car, and I left for Athens.

## Chapter Fifteen

We found out in January of 2005. I was driving to Birmingham, Alabama, the day I got the news. A week earlier, I had driven home to Athens to take Atline to the see a doctor. She had been sick off and on for over a month.

The first healthcare facility I took her to was a clinic. The nurse checked her out and said that she thought it was an infection. They gave her medicine and sent us on our way. After taking Atline home, I left and went back to South Carolina. A few weeks later, my mother called again. She said the medicine hadn't helped Atline at all, and that she may need to go to the hospital. My mother couldn't get Atline to go, and she knew I was the only one that could force her.

I drove back to Athens a little aggravated because

I felt like Atline was being difficult, as usual, and that she would have me drive 3 hours to make her go to the hospital when she could just stop being disobedient and let my mother take her. I walked in the house, and Atline was lying on the sofa, watching television. She was shocked to see me, but you could tell by the look on her face that she knew why I was there.

"Get your ass up and let's go!"

She didn't say a word. She got up off the sofa, went to her room, and got dressed.

Let me tell you about the relationship I have with Atline. From birth, she has always been a sickly child. She had seizures when she was very young, which led to other health complications. She's had a pretty difficult life, being in and out of hospitals most of her childhood. By the time she was 10 or 11, she grew out of most of her health issues, but she's never had a strong, healthy body.

Because of her former conditions, my mother and stepfather always spoiled her rotten. Anything she wanted, anything her heart desired, was hers. If one of her siblings taunted or upset her in any way, we got in *major* trouble. No one was allowed to bother her at all. I've gotten kicked out of the house onto the streets too many times for fussing with Atline. She was spoiled as hell, and the worst thing about it all is that she knew it, and she used it to her advantage.

There were always conflicts growing up in the house with her because she knew you couldn't bother her, and she would harass the shit out of us, including my mother and stepfather.

As she got older, her attitude became so bad that my mother couldn't do anything with her anymore. She wouldn't listen to my mother at all. She wasn't a mean person. She was a very sweet girl, and all the teachers and her friends loved her, but she gave my mother pure hell. I was the only one in the family that Atline would listen to. She knew I was stern and didn't play when it came to her acting out. I loved her to death, but she knew she couldn't play and get over on me like she did our mother. Any time my mother had a problem with Atline, she would always call me to try to resolve it.

When my mother called me to tell me that Atline wouldn't let her take her to the hospital, I knew I was going to have to take a trip to Athens and get her to go, and I wasn't happy about driving that distance.

I've tried to tell my mother over the years that she wasn't helping Atline when she spoiled her and let her have her way. She was only hurting her. My mother would never listen to me. I could not get her to see how it wasn't good for both their relationship and for Atline as an individual. My Mother never put her foot down when it came to Atline, and I wish so badly she had. I can't help but to wonder if she had maybe Atline would still be here with us.

So many times, I told my mother to make sure Atline was getting her routine female checkups, like every woman should get. It was hard for me to know what was going on at my mother's house sometimes, because I lived in another state, and I was always on the road working. I would always express to my mother how important it was for Atline to get checked, especially when she was old enough to hang in the street with her friends and go to clubs. The world is an unpredictable and unsure place for a newcomer, especially if one is not prepared.

Atline wasn't prepared, because she had been sheltered all her life, so when she did hit the streets, she did what any child would do without knowledge or understanding. She ran wild. My mother had a hard time making Atline do anything she asked. When my mother would try to take Atline to get her routine exams, Atline would always get upset and complain about how she didn't want to go and how she was so scared that the exam would hurt. So my mother wouldn't take her.

There were times that I would get so upset with my mother because it never seemed like she understood the importance of Atline getting her exams. She use to tell me that Atline gave her such a fit when it was time to go for the exam that she would say, "forget it." I told her she was making a *big* mistake.

I had other brothers and sisters living in Athens also, but Atline didn't listen to any of them either. There was no use for any of them to even try to talk any sense into Atline. I would try to talk to Atline over the phone and try to make her go with Mom to her exams. She would listen, but as soon as I hung up, she would give my mother a hard time and intimidate my mother into not taking her. I had to be in front of Atline, face to face, in order for her to do what I asked.

The day I made her get off that sofa and go to the hospital with me was the first time we had even considered taking her anywhere other than the local clinic. We thought she just had a persistent infection of some sort. My mother rode with us to the hospital. The doctor checked Atline in as my mother and I stood in the room with her. The doctor removed a sample of her uterine wall and put it in a container that looked like a pill bottle. He told us he would run some tests, and then he sent us home.

The next week, I was driving to Birmingham. I don't even remember why I was driving there, but it was most likely to work. I got a phone call from my mother. She was crying when I picked up the phone. My heart started pounding; I could feel it in my throat. I just listened, not saying anything. Then my mother hung up without saying a word.

I didn't call back. I was trying to prepare myself for the news. She called back again, and when I answered, I still didn't say anything. I just listened. She was crying even harder this time. She hung up again. Finally, I got the guts to call her this time, thinking I had prepared myself for what she was going to tell me. She answered the phone, still crying uncontrollably.

"Buffie, Atline has cancer!" she burst out and promptly hung up.

I couldn't believe what she had just said, but I dared not pick the phone back up and call her again. Her words sank in. My eyes started watering, and my head started pounding. I had the worst headache I had ever experienced, just that quick. I said, "No," out loud in a soft, calm voice. I was driving, so I had to slow down because I couldn't see the road. My eyes were completely full of tears, and my heart felt so much pain that I thought I wasn't going to make it.

I pulled off on the next exit and into the parking lot of a gas station. I cried and cried. I couldn't stop. I didn't even know my eyes could produce so many tears. My phone rang, and it was Judy. I wiped my face, calmed down, and said hello.

"Did you talk to Mom?" she asked. I said yes. I could hear the sorrow in her voice, and I couldn't bear to stay on the phone. I told her I would call her back, hung up, and continued crying.

All I kept asking myself was *why Atline*? Hasn't she been through enough in life? She was just too young for this, and I didn't feel like she deserved it. I know she was a difficult child, but it wasn't her fault. I felt the reason she was unruly and hard to deal with is because she was raised not knowing any different. Atline never had real guidance outside of what she was taught in school. She always got what she wanted, when she wanted it, and there weren't any rules. A child only knows what their surroundings teach them. If Atline had been going to the doctor, getting her yearly exams like most women, then maybe we could have known that she had vaginal cancer at an early stage, and the doctors could have caught it in time.

For the next 10 months until she died, I wanted to blame everyone in the world who didn't listen to me about my sister. Her death hurt me so terribly, and I feel that her life could have been spared and she would still be here with me today, enjoying and sharing my successful life. She didn't get to see all the things that I accomplished since her passing. She did get to see my first music video with G-Unit, my first magazine spread, and my first magazine cover. She used to call or text me every time she saw that "So Seductive" video on TV. It just thrilled her to see her sister on television with 50 Cent and Tony Yayo. If she lived long enough to see me in the film *ATL*, I know for a fact she would have watched that movie about a hundred times by now.

Once Atline got really sick, I tried to stay away from her because it hurt so much to see her like that. I just couldn't handle someone I love having to go through what she went through. I'm not as tough as I try to make myself look. I know that God knows best and I shouldn't question Him, but I was completely dumbfounded as to why He chose Atline to go. I've come to deal with her passing a lot better. My mother hasn't dealt with it too well. She goes to the gravesite a least once a week seems like. Every time I talk to her, she mentions that she just left Atline's grave.

I paid for a large stone with all of our names engraved on it to be placed over the site. I wanted her to know she may be gone off the earth, but we are still with her. With her passing, there are only six siblings left. I never imagined in a thousand years that she would be the first to leave the clan. She was the last to come and the first to go.

Ladies, females, girls, women: *please* get your routine exams. Don't ever sleep on the idea that it can't happen to you, because it can. I can't express how important your health is. I can't tell you what my family went through in the months leading to my sister's death. Her ankles were swollen to the point that she could barely walk. Her bones started breaking. She had to go through treatments that made her feel sicker than if she hadn't been on medication. Eventually, she went blind. Ladies, get your exams and follow up with your doctors. Make no excuses.

I've dedicated this book to my sister, Atline Hardy, who died of ovarian cancer November 19, 2005. Rest in peace, little sister. I love you.

# Chapter Sixteen

The year 2005 will always be one of the busiest years of my life. Although I had Atline on my mind at all times, I felt the need to envelope myself with work. When I became Buffie the Body, the news about my ass spread like the wildfires in California. Everybody wanted to see my ass up close. I had people contacting me left and right wanting to interview me and ask questions. People were really acting like they had never seen a big ass before in their lives. From the radio stations to the magazines, local newspapers to promoters and industry players, *everybody* wanted a piece of the action.

Club owners and promoters started hitting me up to do walk-throughs and club appearances at their special events. Every e-mail I got, I would forward to my assistant. I was thrilled that people wanted to pay me to come to their club and just sit around. When I was dancing, I would have to dance all night long, sometimes completely nude, to make this type of money. Now all I have to do is walk in a club, smile, take photos, talk on the mic, and be there for 1 hour. How easy can that be?

More than women were curious about meeting The Body. Kanye West and I went back and forth that year. He had seen me in *KING* magazine and wanted me to be in one of his upcoming videos. He's incredibly intelligent and was very nice when we exchanged conversation.

Around the same time, I started chating with Busta Rhymes on the phone. A friend, Will, called me up one day and told me that Busta wanted to talk to me. He connected Busta on three-way, and we talked briefly and exchanged numbers. We stayed in touch for months after, and he came to my birthday party in 2007.

I love Busta's music but always thought he was a little cocky. Depending on how a man carries it, cockiness can be very appealing. He mentioned doing one of his music videos, but it never happened because we sort of lost contact after awhile. That's how it normally happens. I'll start off having very laid-back, cool conversations with an industry man. I guess after they see that it never goes any further with me than the occasional phone call, they lose interest and move to the next female. I don't blame them; I'm sure they can find another female that's more fun than I am. They usually don't have much desire for a female who's not into hanging out and partying.

My team and I set my hosting price at a reasonable rate to sit at a club for an hour or two. My rider stated that a promoter would have to fly me and a companion (security or agent) round-trip to the event (only first class if the flight is over 2 hours), provide me security if I wasn't traveling with one, put each of us in a four- or five-star hotel, feed us, provide ground transportation to and from the airport and to and from the club event, and provide transportation and security if I wanted to roam the city and shop. It was that simple!

Requests started rolling in by the truckload. I was on the road five to ten times a month across the United States and Canada. There was never a venue too big or too small, and I didn't care how tiny or rural the town or city was. I didn't turn any money down. If you had the money to book me, agree to my rider requirements, and provide safe conditions, then I'd be there.

I also began hosting and cohosting parties for and with industry celebrities. I hosted a party in Houston at Club Ice Age with Mike Jones. He was nothing like I thought he would be. I expected him to be hood and ghetto as hell, but not at all. Mike and his team were very helpful and nice to me and my people. The club was so packed that I stayed in the DJ booth the entire night with the deejays and Mike.

Mike kept checking on me, making sure I was okay and seeing if I needed anything. He may be from the streets or from the hood, but it didn't show at all to me. He had excellent hosting skills, and his manners were impeccable. Sometimes what you see on TV is not at all how these rappers really are. I took pictures with Mike and once again I was out, back to my hotel.

I've cohosted parties and events with just about everyone you can think of: Young Jeezy, Gucci Mane, Plies, Vivica A. Fox, Boris Kodjoe, G-Unit, Allen Iverson, Morris Chestnut, Ciara, Twister, 8Ball and MJG, Mike Jones, Paul Wall, Randy Moss, Luke, Big Tigger, Trey Songz, T-Pain, Yung Joc, Common, Too Short, Irv Gotti, Jalen Rose, Micheal Jordan, Jermaine Dupree, Trina, Shaq, and many, many more.

I can honestly say every celebrity I've worked with was mad cool! I couldn't believe how I never had a bad experience, and none of them left a bad taste in my mouth. Most of them seem just as glad to finally meet Buffie the Body as I was to meet them. They were always willing to take pictures with me, and if I was shooting a video like I was the first year of my career, they were willing to speak on camera. I've kept in touch with many of them after events.

I was getting booked so much, it was like I was a rapper or singer. It was off one plane, on another. I was traveling so much that I would forget what city I was in or where I just came from when it was time to pick my luggage up in baggage claim. The agent assisting me would ask me what city I just flew in from, and I'd say, "I have no idea!"

It was crazy but a blessing. I was getting money, staying

in nice hotels, eating at five-star restaurants, shopping, my fans were sending me gifts, and my Web site was doing well. At the same time, I was meeting and networking with countless celebrities and couldn't turn one way without some industry player reach out to shake my hand, give me a hug, or ask to take a picture with me.

I was hosting a party in Philly back in 2006. Sundy Carter, a model, was having a birthday party. It was packed as hell. You couldn't even move in that club. I noticed that Irv Gotti and I were in VIP together.

He had a very inviting personality. He smiled and laughed and enjoyed the party like everyone else was. He gave me a hug when I made my way over to him. We took a few photos together. There were groupies everywhere trying to get to Irv. I just shook my head. I'm so used to seeing this every time I'm in VIP with a male celebrity. I can't believe how desperate these women are. They have no shame in their game whatsoever. All they wanted to do is get Irv to notice them on the chance that they could go home with him.

As my hosting continued, I was floored at the idea that I was making more money than I would have ever thought I could make, and not only did it actually belong to me, but I had earned it myself. I had a travel agency who would book my flights, and I worked with several booking agencies out of New York, Philly, and Atlanta. Amina Diop has been around since the summer of 2005. She was technically my assistant, but she helped with *everything*, so she was really like a manager. She became my best friend, and one of the few friends I've made in this industry. It's extremely difficult to trust people in this business, so I kept my team and my circle very close and tight.

What was even more difficult than trusting people was trying to keep niggas from touching my ass when I was hosting. People could not keep their hands off my booty. It was like my butt was a hand magnet. My motto was, "If you touch my ass, I'm going to touch you," and that was how it was. Most of the time, I would have security with me when I walked around the club, but it didn't matter to some dudes because they would still reach their hand around security and try to touch me. Sometimes people would come to me and ask me in a very polite way if they could touch my ass. Rarely, and only if I'm in a good mood or having a good night, would I'd let them. When I allow it, it's with mostly women. Guys don't always know how to act when they see a big booty. As time went on, people stopped trying to touch my butt for the most part. Of course, there's always going to be someone acting a fool. People smile when they see me, ask to take a picture with me, and they want a hug.

There will always be a female who can't handle my success and wants to hate in the club. They want the fame, they want the nice clothes, they want the success, and they want the attention. Can I really believe that some women just really hate me? No, I know they don't, because you can't hate somebody that you don't even know.

One night, I was in Chicago hanging out with a friend of mine, Deshawn. We were in a club in downtown Chicago, chillin' in the VIP with some of his other friends. They were drinking, and I was just sitting, watching the scene. I noticed this group beside us acting all wild and shit. There were about 10 girls and six guys. They were all drunk as hell.

After a while, the females started dancing wild and getting closer and closer to me. There was a ledge behind me, and they got up on the ledge and stated dancing over my head. I told the security to remove them from the ledge. He made them move once, but they kept coming back like there was no other place to dance but behind me. I know they wanted me to say something to them so I could give them a reason to start a fight, but I said nothing. I felt like I had too much to lose if I got in a fight with these hood rats, and by the way they looked and the way they were dressed, you could tell *they* had *nothing* to lose.

Once again, I told the security to remove the girls from around me, and the security made them move again. Then all of a sudden, one of the girls, pretending to be more drunk than she really was, fell on our table and broke a few of our glasses, spilling wine on my boots. I jumped up, and my friend grabbed the girl and pushed her away from us. She staggered back and fell. One of the guys in her party saw what happened and jumped up to defend her. Deshawn got into a scuffle with him. Everyone started beefing, and the crowd got out of control. The two parties were then separated, and the other party was asked to leave. I told management and security they didn't have to leave because I was out, and I grabbed my things.

I can pick a group of haters out from any crowd. I try to avoid people that are obviously troublemakers everywhere they go; they have nothing to lose. I've had men at the club who get mad at me and want to kick my ass because I wouldn't take a picture with them or they thought I was intentionally ignoring them. Guys can be really sensitive, especially the ones who try so hard and pretend that nothing fazes them. I do try to accommodate my fans as much as possible; they are the reason for my success. Sometimes I don't feel like taking pictures if I'm at a club and I'm just chillin' and not working. Every once in awhile, my fans don't understand that I'm human and like everyone else, I need my space.

Another tough thing about hosting was the traveling. I never liked airplanes because I get motion sickness. I would be sick as hell sometimes when I landed in the different cities. I would have to go straight to my room and lie down until my head was right. I would be so dizzy and nauseous. I wish I had a big tour bus so I wouldn't have to get on a plane!

I have learned how to handle myself well on the road. At first, I was shy to speak my mind to editors, stylists, promoters, and agents because I was new to the modeling game. Now, if I don't like the way something is going, then

then somebody needs to change it and quick or else I'm not doing anything until it's done. One thing that used to get under my skin is the questions and the expectations that some of these promoters had when they would inquire about booking me. Half of the promoters wanted to know if I would be wearing swimwear or lingerie to the event. *Hold up! WHAT did he just ask?* Why on earth would I wear that type of attire to a club or event? It was almost insulting to hear how adamant some of these promoters were about me coming to the club in skimpy outfits.

Come to find out they thought that since they see me in all those magazines with my ass out that they assume that's how I would show up at their event. I tried to explain to them that what they see in the magazines are photo shoots and that's what I'm supposed to wear. There's no way in hell I'm coming to any club or event in a damn swimsuit. No exceptions!

We were getting so many requests for me to wear a swimsuit that we had to add a clause in my contract and rider:

> *Buffie always wears appropriate clothing to events. Yes, the outfit will be fashionable. No, the outfit will not include lingerie or a bathing suit. Buffie will not, under any circumstances, wear a bathing suit to a hosting event.*

I would get disgusted when they would keep asking if

I would come in swimwear. Some were even willing to pay what they had to just to get me at their event wearing a bathing suit, but still I refused. It got to the point where if anyone said anything to me about wearing a fuckin' swimsuit, I was going to be very nasty and rude to them. My assistant and my booking agencies stopped letting me know when a promoter would ask about me wearing swimwear because they already knew what type of mood it would put me in, and I would want to get on the phone with the promoter who had the audacity to ask me that question.

Promoters had even started inquiring about me dancing at their events. *Damn, this shit just don't stop!*

"Hell, no, I can't dance at your event. That's a stripper's job, and I'm not a stripper!"

It took a while, at least a year or two, to get people to stop asking me to dance or wear swimsuits to the clubs. It was a long battle, but I completely understood that I had to go through that phase in my life in order to grow as an industry professional. People don't let you live your rocky past down easily, and I know this too well now. Instead of people being happy that I overcame my past and aimed towards a bright future, they always try to throw you under the bus. I look back on that and laugh now because I know I'm so far away from that lifestyle and I knew it would follow me well after I had quit, so I have to take the good with the bad and move forward. People used to tell me that I could really rack up the money in strip clubs now. That's all well and good, but

but no thanks.

All year round, I was juggling hosting, shooting for magazines, keeping up with my Web site, and taking care of my growing pool of incredible fans. I was a model hustler, that's for damn sure. In time, however, my influence would radiate out past men and embrace women. I would go from urban model to role model, one of the greatest honors I've experienced to this day.

# Chapter Seventeen

I was in Memphis, Tennessee, at the airport checking
my e-mail when I received a note from the production
staff at the *Tyra Banks Show*. It was March 2008. I was
on my way to Hattiesburg, Mississippi, to host an event.
I had a layover in Memphis, so I was checking my e-mail
on my laptop. The note said that they wanted me to give
them a call or e-mail them back and let them know if I
would be interested in being on the show.

I wasn't going to get excited until I knew what the
show was about. I say this because the *Michael Baisden
Show* had e-mailed me last year. I was thrilled, only to
find out that the show I was asked to appear for was about
former strippers. I was hesitant to go on, because at the
time, I didn't want to talk about my past life as a stripper
and I didn't know if they would try to make the show

uplifting or make me look like I wasn't shit because I used to be a dancer. I decided to turn the offer down, and I'm still happy with my choice.

When I don't feel right about something, I leave it alone. When the *Tyra Banks Show* got back to me and said the show would focus on helping females feel more secure about having a big booty and to embrace their curves, I was pumped! This show would be right up my alley.

I told them that I would love to come on the show, and they booked my hotel and flight. They said that they would have hair and makeup if I needed it, but I still didn't trust anyone to do my hair or makeup. I flew my hairstylist, Javon Pinellas, from Atlanta, and my makeup artist, George McKenney, from Detroit. Amina, my right hand, was there, and my Web designer joined as well.

My grammar was what I was most nervous about being on Tyra. I didn't want to sound uneducated on national TV, so I made sure I practiced what I was going to say that week prior to going on the show. I'm always using my team to help me with my speech when I need it. I've always thought I had horrible grammar, and my vocabulary is weak. Over the last 3 years, I've been working on both areas extensively. I took a class to improve in these areas, and I go to the bookstore a lot and read books on these subjects.

When I got to New York, it was still a little cold, even though it was the middle of April. I checked into my hotel, and my hairstylist came over to get started.

When we arrived at the studio the next morning, we went straight to my dressing room. Javon and George just put some finishing touches on my hair and makeup, because they had already fixed me up before I left the hotel. The producers had told me to make sure I wore something that would show my curves, so I put on some nicely fitted jeans and a yellow spring top with ruffled short sleeves. The first thing the producers told me when they met me was that I was so pretty in person. I was already used to hearing that, but it never hurts to hear it again and again, especially right before you appear on national television.

One of the production staff members came into my room and told me exactly what the show would be about and what questions Tyra would be asking me. She explained to me that I wouldn't be on the stage but maybe 10 minutes, if that, and after the interview, we could leave.

During Tyra's introduction, they had me and two other ladies standing on stage with our backs to the audience. As Tyra walked around the stage talking, she slapped each female on the booty except me. When Tyra made it over to where I was standing, she clamped down on both of my ass cheeks. It stunned me, but I couldn't help but laugh. I guess everyone else thought it was funny, too, because I heard the audience giggle.

When it was time to actually go out on stage and do my interview, I walked out as Tyra announced me. I turned around, showed the audience what I love and embrace, and then I sat down. There was another female who sat next to me. I don't remember her name, but I had never seen her in any videos or magazines. I don't know where they found her, but the production crew didn't have anything nice to say about her at all. She was overweight, her hair wasn't fixed, and she didn't have her makeup done. I sort of felt sorry for her because she was such a nice girl.

Production admitted that they had made a mistake by putting her on the show. They were very displeased with her overall appearance. I asked them how they found her, and they said they saw some photos of her, but she didn't look in person like she did in the photos she submitted. I told them airbrushing was like plastic surgery. Since they had flown her in, I guess they didn't have a choice but to use her.

Honestly, I didn't like the fact that they had her sitting beside me on the stage. I only say this because I pride myself in taking care of my appearance. I get facials, I keep my hair, I exercise, I try to watch what I eat, and I visit day spas now on a regular basis. For me to be on the *Tyra Banks Show* was a dream and an accomplishment, and to have me sit on national television beside a female who obviously didn't give a damn about how she looked made me upset. Out of all the beautiful "known" urban models that they could have chosen to be on the show with me, they chose *this* female.

After the show aired, so many people asked me in disgust who in the world was the woman sitting next to me. I felt like the fact that she was even on the show might have negatively influenced viewers' perspectives on who I was and what I was all about.

Outside of the other woman, the show went well. Tyra asked me about my problems with being thin, how I gained weight, and my diet and exercise. Tyra was a very nice and professional host. I love her so much because of her accomplishments throughout her career. I think she's a very hardworking woman. I don't know anything about her personal life because I don't follow the gossip and I could care less. I just love what she stands for, and the fact that she's a black woman trying to make it in this world. People told me she would have a horrible attitude and she would try to belittle me and make me look like a fool on TV, but she didn't come close to doing any of that. She asked all the right questions.

There were two other girls on the show who didn't like the fact that they had big butts. They felt insecure about their booties, and the other guest and I were there to show them how to love their curves and their bodies. They didn't even have big butts to me. They had more hips than they could ever have junk in their trunk, and their hips weren't even very big. I thought they were clowns and just wanted to be on the show. Tyra should have hired me to cast the guests for that show! That show's ratings would have been out the roof. I know what a big ass is supposed to look like, and I know what a flat ass looks like. I was the only one on that stage who had a big booty.

I had never considered myself a role model before the show. The whole time I've been in this industry, I've been doing me. Girls tell me all the time that I'm their idol and they look up to me and want to be like me. I'm honored that there's someone who wants to be like me, but I didn't come in this industry trying to be some sort of hero or trying to enlighten and empower others. I was just tired of dancing and living the way that I was. My life was going nowhere fast, and I was ready for a change. My lifestyle was beginning to make me unhappy; I wanted and desired more. I wasn't broke, on drugs, or abused. I didn't have a house full of kids and five baby daddies. I didn't create any limitations that held me back in life. I realize now that these are reasons young ladies look up to me. Not everyone can avoid temptations, stay true to themselves and not men, not hate women, while still focusing on personal success.

No, I didn't go to college, but I had my imagination and ambition, and on top of that, I was a hustler armed with common sense and street smarts. I've always considered myself close to God, and we talk often. I just needed that one break—to gain weight—and it was on! I've come to realize that I enlighten women with my story, but I'm still overwhelmed by the thought that some consider me a role model.

No one is perfect; we've all made, and will make, mistakes, but my mistakes were never significant enough to hold me back from doing anything I wanted to do in this

this world. The sky is my limit, and I'm just beginning. So, if I'm a role model for dancers who wish to get out of the strip game, girls who want big butts, ladies who want to be on the cover of magazines, females who want to do music videos, or women who just want to be successful, then I appreciate the title and the thought.

I've grown into an independent woman over the years, and I'm not into what the crowd is into. I'm into what I'm into, and that works for me. I'm continuing to build a better life for myself. Not for a man, not for a family member, not for the industry moneymakers. For myself. I want women to see me, read my story, and know that they can change their lives too. I'm a woman who took shit and made it into a decent life, and still, I'm not satisfied until I reach the top. I don't know which female celebrities slept around to get to the top—maybe Tyra, Jennifer Lopez, or maybe even Beyoncé—but that's not my style, and who did and didn't isn't important to me. What's important is that they made it and they continue to grow and shine and be independent women that we all look up to. I'm sure they had to go through bullshit, with niggas trying to fuck and a lot of rejections, but they didn't let it stop them. No one is perfect. I have to set my own path and make wise and professional decisions and not let this industry devour me like it has so many other ladies.

# Chapter Eighteen

"Oh, wow, you look so much better in person!"

After hearing this comment one too many times, I finally asked myself, "Why don't I look as appealing in the magazines as I do in person?"

I've learned that when it comes to putting me in a magazine, stylists, photographers, designers, and editors are only concerned with my ass. Apparently, my fans look close enough to know that magazines certainly don't concentrate on my face. Magazine editors want the perfect ass shot. They didn't give a hoot about my smile, my eyes, my lips, my nose, or anything else. All they want is that ass shot, because in all honesty, the ass shot is what sells the magazine. Who can blame them? A voluptuous woman on a cover will outsell thin women on the cover in the urban industry any day. You can put a magazine with a slim girl with a pretty face and no ass on a shelf, and then you can put a girl with no face or head at all but a small waist and a fat ass and the men are going to buy that second magazine before they buy the other. That's just men.

There have been times that I've seen photos of myself in magazines I didn't think looked good at all. Sometimes the makeup is not how you like, sometimes your hair is crazy, and sometimes the pose is just off-point. A lot of things have to be right to make a good photo. I know what makes me look pretty, and no one knows better than I do. I know what hairstyles, makeup, and colors compliment me, and I hate when a shoot staff doesn't listen when I try to tell them. Like I said, in the beginning of my career, I was too scared to say anything because I didn't want them to not do the shoot if I was being difficult. Now, since I'm known around the urban entertainment block, I speak up when I don't like something.

I started an epidemic with the big booties and dark skin. It seems as if features like mine weren't accepted by mainstream media and this industry until I came around. Even in 2005, there wasn't anyone like me. It's possible this is why I was so successful. Maybe people were tired of looking at the same slim, light-skinned chicks. I feel like I brought something new to the game; I brought change and diversity, and the world loved it.

The only model I've known to come close to having my features and skin color is Ki Toy Johnson, from back in 2003. Ki Toy's name didn't go as far as mine, and she was never as big as me, but I would definitely compare my image to hers. She was dark-skinned and thick, and I thought she was so beautiful. I thought she was the perfect woman. I never knew why she didn't stay around long, but she didn't. I think I picked up where she left off, and I didn't look back. I made this into a career. Other than Ki Toy and me, there weren't any other girls.

Of course, now, there are so many models with big butts and small waists, but I feel like the market is so overly saturated with big booty girls that there isn't the same excitement for it like it used to be. I was the first to break the mainstream with my looks, and after me, it wasn't a big shock anymore. If you've seen one big ass, you've seen them all. I'm not telling females this to discourage them and tell them not to keep trying to break into this industry, but I am saying it to let them know that you need other things to fall back on if the big booty thing is not working for you. I'm just keeping it real, and I'm not trying to hate.

The new models, especially the ones with the big booties, are always asking my advice on how to get noticed and get a name in this industry. I always tell them to not just depend on the fact that they have a big booty to make it in this industry. Yes, I admit that my ass was my main reason behind my success, but everyone can't expect it to happen as easily for them as it was for me. I was one in a million at the time.

At one time, I couldn't pass a female without her saying some awkward shit. Girls don't hate on me as much as they used to, but there are, and will always be, some that can't grasp the fact that I am who I am, and they can't change that. I've banked on my ass for years now, but I was smart enough to use what I've learned over the years to become diverse and know my ass wouldn't always be there to save me forever.

For 4 years straight, I was either on the cover of magazines, in music videos, or somewhere showing my ass. I'm sure people think that I can't do anything but pose for the camera and shake my ass. My future isn't planned around proving them wrong; I live for me, and I had to prove to myself that I have the ability to do other things—and here I am.

Even a model who I consider a major player in the industry had ill feelings towards me when I finally met her. I don't consider but three models to be top dogs in this industry: Melyssa Ford, Vida Guerra, and Gloria Velez. These three models were doing their thing way before I even thought about modeling. I consider these ladies icons. I've heard rumors that Vida and Melyssa have said negative things about me. Now is it true? I don't know, so to me, they're just rumors.

I met Vida in the beginning of 2008 in Los Angeles on the set of a reality show. She was cool as hell. I couldn't believe how easy it was to be around her, and how laid-back she was. She and I hit it off well. She didn't seem like an airhead, like some of the models I've met, and she was open about her career in terms of her experiences in the industry. She wasn't stuck up, and she wasn't standoffish. Since the show, we've kept in touch. If she's fake, she didn't appear fake to me.

I met Melyssa at the end of 2006 in Los Angeles as well. We were both shooting for *KING* magazine's 5-year anniversary issue. Melyssa had the worst attitude I had ever experienced, from not only a model, but from anyone I had ever met in the entire industry. I couldn't believe such a pretty girl would have such a nasty and disgusting disposition, and it was apparent that everyone at the shoot could tell she was having a problem. She was walking around, swiftly slamming doors with her nose in the air and a frown on her face. No one was talking to her but the crew she came with, and she wasn't talking to anyone but them as well. She didn't speak to me once during the entire shoot.

Trina, Mýa, and Reagan Gomez, who were all at the shoot as well, were so nice and pleasant to me. But not Melyssa. I couldn't believe all these years I had looked up to her and praised her on all her accomplishments, and when I finally meet her, she was incredibly rude. She would make snide comments about me when someone would mention my name around her. I had never said anything negative about her, so I knew that wasn't the reason she had issues with me. When it was all said and done, she just didn't like sharing the spotlight with me, or anyone else, for that matter. She didn't think I deserved the attention that the world has given me, and she sure didn't agree with me being established enough in the industry to be in the same magazine with the same credits and regard as her.

One of the staff at the shoot eventually told me flat-out that Melyssa had a problem with me being there. After a while, news had spread through the shoot and everyone had gotten the word that Melyssa was upset because I was at the shoot and, in a nutshell, she wanted me gone. I had always wanted to be on the cover of *KING* magazine after breaking into the business, so I wasn't going to let her mess this up for me. I finished the photo shoot and left. I just didn't have the time or energy for that childish nonsense. I don't know how she feels about me today, but I still don't hold any dislike for her. It is what it is.

For every hater, I have hundreds of supporters. I'm always getting shout-outs from men in the industry. Jamie Foxx got in touch with me multiple times, asking if I would fly to LA to speak on his talk show. He was always very kind and supportive.

I've been given love from Big Boi, whom I met on the set of *ATL*; I ran into Lil John in LA at the airport once, and we've kept in touch since; Young Jeezy, who I met in Virginia in 2005, is one of the friendliest people I've met; I've run into Twista multiple times, and he's always been very polite and somewhat quiet. The list could go on: Boris

Kodjoe, Plies, Pall Wall, Luke, Big Tigger, Young Joc, Jermaine Dupree, Ludacris, and so many more industry men have all been nothing less than respectful and welcoming. Luda and I met at the Kentucky Derby. He was actually one of the first rappers I started talking on the phone with. He was always very friendly, and I think he's an incredibly talented artist.

I've met many women in the industry also who are simply fantastic people. I met Vivica Fox in the fall of 2006 at a party in Detroit. We shared a VIP section with Morris Chestnut. Vivica was so vibrant and full of life. She always smiled, and she loves her fans. She took photos with everyone that asked, and she didn't act like a celebrity at all. She was so down-to-earth and nice. She didn't seem like a fake person like you would think most celebrities of her caliber would be. It surprised me how open and inviting she was.

Morris was sort of quiet but always pleasant. He was much smaller and shorter than I thought he would be, but still very handsome. The women were going crazy over him, and I could tell that he was probably used to that.

I met Ciara at a party in Dekalb, Illinois. It was cold that night. I was the host along with a woman from the local radio station. The event took place at a local school. So many people were there! Thousands of kids were present. The radio personality and I were on stage before Ciara came out. It was my job to talk to the crowd and keep them occupied until she was ready to perform.

This was my first big event, and I was so nervous, standing on that stage under those bright lights in front of all those kids. When Ciara was finally ready to come out, I met her back behind the stage. She gave me a big bright smile and a friendly wave before rushing out. I stood backstage for about 15 minutes and watched her perform. The kids loved her! She definitely knows how to get the crowd hyped, and she can dance her ass off! She's a very pretty girl and appears to be very shy and humble.

Regardless of how I'm treated, I know to just keep moving. I've always embraced my shape and my skin color. My skin tone helped tremendously with my popularity after I was given a chance to shine. I can't think of any girls with my shape or color in the urban modeling industry that really stole the spotlight like I did. You would see them here or there but not really up-front like you did the light-skinned models. To be honest, I really didn't think it was even possible to do what I've done in the last 4 years because of my skin tone, regardless of how much I've loved it.

I've heard a million times that I'm cute to be so dark, and I don't know if I should take that as an insult or not. Beauty is in the eye of the beholder. What one person may think is ugly, the next person may think is beautiful. I've heard comments from other models like, "I'm prettier than Buffie, and my ass is bigger than hers!" I even had a model e-mail me and say, "You're ugly and dark-skinned, and you need

need to move over and let this light-skinned girl take over." I just laugh and keep it moving. There is no one on this earth that can convince me that I'm ugly. Yes, I have deep-mocha skin, and I love it to death. I've had men come up to me and tell me that they don't normally date dark black women, but they would make an exception for me! I should be honored, shouldn't I, that my ass has given me light-skinned privileges?

I got breast implants in 2007. I guess no one has really noticed, because they were too busy looking at my ass. I've never liked my breasts because I didn't think they were full enough. I had wanted breast implants for about 8 years but was always too scared to get them. I was afraid that I might get a bad boob job that couldn't be corrected. If you're a dancer and your breast implant procedure goes wrong, everyone is going to know, and your ability to bring in the dough decreases. When I was finally able to stop dancing, I decided to take the risk and get my breasts done.

I did my research in Jamaica when I was there for my *Smooth* magazine photo shoot. I stayed at a resort where the people walked around nude all day and all night, so I saw a lot of titties. For every set of breasts I saw that I thought looked fantastic, I would get Amina to go and ask the woman if I could talk to her about her boob job. The women were always very willing to talk to me about their surgery, the aftercare, and the final results. They would even make me touch and squeeze them so I could feel how soft and natural they were. These women were so satisfied and happy about their breasts; you could tell just by how they walked around topless with confidence. I was so amped by the time I left Jamaica that I made my appointment as soon as I got back home. My family and friends were against the surgery, but I was just doing me, and I'm so glad I did. I love them!

I watch plastic surgery shows on TV all the time; my favorite is *Dr. 90210*. I love how those women are so happy when they leave the doctor's office with their new additions. I'm really scared to touch anything on my face because I won't be able to hide it if it doesn't come out right. I would love a Stacey Dash nose or Robin Given's jawbone structure, but I'm really scared to go through with it and probably won't ever do it.

I really wish someone would come out with some type of procedure to get rid of cellulite. I would be the first bitch in line, right next to Tyra Banks! I've tried lotions, but that shit does *not* work. I should have known it didn't work because it was too easy to find in the stores, and the shelves were fully stocked with it.

To any female wishing to get plastic surgery: to each her own. If you think it would make you feel better to have a bigger booty, and you've tried everything, then go for it. Anything that will truly improve how you feel about yourself, go for it. You can best believe I did my research, and I suggest you do the same. Being beautiful definitely helps your self-esteem, so if you think your nose is too big for your face and you were teased all your life, then change it if that makes you feel better. I hear so much talk about different celebrities getting work done like Vivica A. Fox, Alicia Keys, Halle Berry, and so on. It's so obvious that Lil Kim had surgery, and I haven't heard one person say that it looks good. I think she was so pretty before her surgery.

I'm confident in saying that I was the first rich-skinned urban model to have a solo cover of *KING* magazine, the first dark-chocolate urban model to be granted a *BlackMen* magazine SSX Issue, the first dark-skinned model to win *XXL* magazine's Eye Candy of the Year, and the first dark-skinned model with 45-inch hips to be the featured video girl in any of G-Unit's releases. Not to mention the probable fact that I'm the first dark-toned video girl and model with 45-inch hips to do anything major in this industry, and that's so sad.

My future goal is to pose for *Playboy* magazine. I would consider it one of my greatest accomplishments because of my skin tone and my size. I know more and more white men are becoming aware of black female bodies, and they are loving it. Even white women today want to be shaped like black females. You have more white women getting butt implants than you do black women.

*Playboy* is so tasteful and many big-name celebrities have been on their cover. You're respected if you make the cover of *Playboy*. I would not do *Hustler* magazine because they get raw. In my opinion, it's just not tasteful.

I feel like any "white" publication that's tasteful that would feature me would be great. I don't think it will happen any time soon, but who knows. It's hard for black models with my shape to get mainstream work because either my ass is too big and it scares corporate America, or they feel like I'm too fat. White people are still not accepting girls that are shaped like me into their world. I don't think you will see a thick female with a big booty in clothing ads, beer ads, mainstream commercials, or acting in a major movie. We have Jennifer Hudson, who is absolutely stunning, but not many other thick females can be added to the list.

Now when I say, "big booty," I'm not talking Beyoncé or JLo booties, because I don't consider their butts large enough to ever attract negative attention in certain markets. I think Beyoncé has more hips than ass. She's never had an ass that poked out and was super phat. Beyoncé is thick, but she has wide hips with a wide ass. JLo's booty sticks out way farther than Beyoncé's. Still, these mainstream women don't have asses like urban models today do in these music videos.

Back in 2005 when I did my first music video with Tony Yayo, I remember BET ended up editing most of my ass out. I remember this like it was yesterday. It was a day during the week that the video was airing the first time. I was so excited that day I was calling everyone I knew, telling them to watch me. I had everyone glued in front of their TVs, waiting for my big debut. I was so nervous because I had never been on TV before and I wanted to look perfect.

When *Rap City* finally came on, my heart was beating like crazy. My palms were sweaty, and I couldn't sit still for shit. When the video finally began, I sat there studying it like I was studying for a class assignment. I wouldn't, and couldn't, take my eyes off the screen.

When the video finally went off and my heart started back beating, I was a little upset. No one had told me that the video would be edited like it was. I know that a good number of my scenes had been edited to show me from the waist up, or they had been deleted altogether. I was hot! I called Jason, a friend who worked for BET at that time, and asked him what was up.

"What the fuck? Why did they edit out my ass, Jason?"

"BET is funny like that like," Jason replied. "They're trying to be real careful these days about their image because of how much negative feedback and media they've been getting about the girls in the music videos."

"But Jason, I wasn't dancing in a lewd way, and I didn't have on short shorts or a bathing suit. I had on a tasteful black dress that came to my knees!" I protested. "Look at some of the bitches in these videos with bathing suits on, jiggling their asses on the beach and in front of the camera, and they let that shit slide!"

Jason just held the phone, not knowing what to say.

I still have black people in America who can't accept the size of my ass or my body shape, so you can imagine how hard it is for white America to accept me. They won't even put any magazines with me on the cover in the checkout aisles of supermarkets. Can you imagine a white couple and their child seeing my ass on the cover of a magazine in the place where they're buying their groceries? They would consider the size of my ass pornographic, and I've never done porn in my life!

My ass does have its disadvantages. I have to buy jeans with a long inseam. I can never walk in a store and buy jeans or pants and wear them the same day. All my bottoms, unless they have elastic in the waist or a drawstring, absolutely have to be altered in the waist before I can wear them—*all* of them. You can imagine how last-minute shopping for pants and jeans will never go well for me. My last-minute shopping consists of dresses and one-piece jumpsuits that are stretchy or spandex. I just can't wear a lot of things. Having a big ass can make a nice conservative outfit look ghetto as hell! It happens to me all the time. The outfits look so nice and ladylike—until I put them on, then "classy" can quickly go on out the window. In the end, it's my ass, and I wished for it, and believe me, it's worth it.

Parts of society don't consider dark women "stunning," but I know a lot of beautiful, deep-toned sisters, and I know some ugly-ass light-skinned females. Sometimes society doesn't give rich-chocolate sisters a chance because we're just automatically categorized as being ugly. I'm sure there are thousands of people who think that I'm not pretty enough to have had this much attention, but there are millions who support me and think that I deserve it.

# Chapter Nineteen

The e-mail above is real. That's certainly not the first
message on the subject, and it won't be the last. I
don't only get them from women; I get them from men,
too.

I have a close relationship with God and always have. I say grace before I eat, and I talk and pray to God often. I haven't been to church in years, but that doesn't have keep me from having Him in my life. If you love and praise God, then that's wonderful, but I hate when someone tries to tell me how to have a relationship with God or how to praise Him. I believe in God, and I was raised in the church. God loves me, and I know He does. My life is good because of Him. I can't allow anyone on the streets to tell me that God doesn't bless me because I'm a model or because I used to be a dancer. He has blessed me and watched over me my entire life, and He will never stop and turn His back on me—like a lot of people in this world have.

I can always talk to God when I can't talk to anyone else, and He listens. I pray for guidance and strength every day to tackle what life brings me and the people that are close to me. Without God, my life wouldn't be as blessed as it is now, and it's only going to get better. As God has blessed me, I've blessed the people around me. I've paid mortgages, purchased cars for people, loaned money, paid for health care, taken people on vacations, paid utilities, and the whole nine yards.

I don't ask for much; I just want to be happy and successful. So I tell people to stop trying to tell me how my relationship with God is supposed to be. I also hate when people try to make me go to church. They act as if there is no other way to be close to God unless you're in church every week. I disagree with that, and no one will ever be able to change my mind.

I personally disagree with a lot of things I see when it comes to churches and attending church. Some of the most judgmental people I've ever met in my life were people who were heavily into church. I get disgusted when someone who attends church all the time pushes me to go. I always appreciate the thought and the gesture, but my temperature starts boiling when they become persistent and won't leave me alone about it. Every time you see them, that's all they want to talk about. They're constantly calling you, leaving messages on your voice mail about how important it is to be in church. That's when I have to tell them to leave me alone. Don't try to pressure me into doing anything just because you think that's what I need to be doing.

I know people who go to church and pay their church dues faithfully every single Sunday, but they can't even afford to pay their bills, and their lights get turned off, and their car is barely running. You see the preacher living in a five-million-dollar home and driving a $100,000 car. If he's living like that, then everyone who attends that church and gives their hard-earned money should be living well, too. That's how I see it, and no one can change my mind. Everyone should be equal in those churches.

How can a leader of a church live like a king, but half of the congregation is barely making ends meet? I've never in my life thought that a preacher should get paid to preach. I think it should be volunteer work or something they do as a hobby. I feel like you should be able to get paid doing anything, but not teaching the Word of God. Yes, I know the church may need repairs, and the church's utilities and bills need to be paid, but that's it! I personally feel that being a preacher should be something you do on the strength because you love and worship God, not to profit and live like a kingpin while your congregation lives like a bunch of crackheads. Like I said, I disagree with a lot of things that go on in churches, but it's just my personal opinion, and everyone is entitled to one, so don't try to change mine.

I know what's right and what's wrong. I know and believe in helping people and doing the right thing. I don't feel the need to always get paid or a need to get something in return when I help people or give them advice. I don't need a person or a Bible to guide me in life, because I know when I'm doing something that's not right. I'm at peace in my relationship with God, and I don't need anyone to vouch for that. I understand that people go to church to fill a void in their lives and to join in fellowship with their fellow Christians. However, I never understood why it is deemed necessary for me to go to church to prove that I believe in God. One has nothing to do with the other. I have a fantastic relationship with the Creator, and I don't feel as though I have to make a preacher hundreds of thousands of dollars richer to receive blessings from God. Come on, now, you have to admit that shit sounds crazy.

I am not saying that preachers are not good motivational speakers or leaders. All I am saying is if they're living richly off of the money their followers break their backs for, their congregations should be balling before the preacher, that's for damn sure! They should all be able to feed their families, have nice vehicles, and have profitable careers. No one in their congregations should be struggling, given that the preachers drive Bentleys and travel by private jets. Okay, okay, if I am losing some of you with these comments, check out the Web sites of some of these large churches. You can have your "donation" automatically deducted from your checking account! Isn't it so convenient that God has a bank account that your money can be directly wired into? Man, I'm in the wrong business.

I have met some of the most hypocritical people that claim they're a child of God. Me, I just choose to worship and am spiritual on my own with my loved ones and God. I just don't believe in the bullshit that's associated with some of these churches. Yeah, I said it, sue me. Judge me if you like, but it won't change my mind.

# Chapter Twenty

They try to come to my room after the club, and I would shut it down quick. Isn't shit going on here! With the haters and supporters come the booty callers. But unless you're calling to do business professionally and without expecting "favors," then I can't help you.

There have been a few celebrities that have called me at two or three in the morning, asking me where I was and if I could come hang out. Even if I were in their city, I would say, "No, I'm home," and the conversation would end abruptly.

"You know I'm a groupie for you, right?"

"Oh, really?" I said blushing, unable to keep a straight face.

"Every time I open a magazine, I see you in it. You're doing your thang."

"Thank you."

That was our first conversation. He was a rapper, quickly moving up the ranks. He went on to ask me if I ever go to Atlanta and when we were going to hang out. I told him I don't go to Atlanta much, even though I was lying. After that first conversation, he started texting me and calling me all the time.

He texted me and asked me where I was one evening. I told him I was in Greensboro, hosting a party. He then asked me to come and see him, and I told him I wouldn't be able to because I was busy. He really expected me to drive to Atlanta from Greensboro to see him! He was wrong on that! He must be used to girls breaking their necks to come and hang out with him. I never replied to him, and he stopped calling for a while.

He again called me out of the blue one day and asked me about doing his next video. I told him I would have to get paid.

"Well, how much will you charge me to do my video?"

"Twenty-five hundred."

"Damn, girl, you're expensive! What can you do on that price for me?"

"What you mean? That isn't a lot of money," I tried to explain to him. I told him that I would talk to my team and get back with him, but I never did. All that fuckin' money he has, and he wants me to do a video for nothing? I'm sure there are a lot of females that would have jumped at the chance to be in this artist's video, but not me! Ain't no way in hell I was going to do that!

He knew that I was a video girl, but he would never offer a spot in a video. He just wanted to sleep with me. That's why I get so disgusted with some of these dudes. They can pick up the phone when they want to fuck or when they see me in a magazine, but when it's time to make some money, why don't they call me then? Oh, I know why! They always call the girls that they're already fucking or the ones that they think they can fuck. Why not? Shouldn't they want a female around them who's willing to fuck, drink, and smoke with them after the video shoot?

Most rappers thought I was a waste of time after the first dozen phone calls, and I was, in most cases. Take Lil Wayne, for instance. Everyone loves Lil Wayne. I'm glad he's doing so well in the industry. I don't agree with the drugs and wouldn't hang out with him if he ever thought I was down to fuck, drink, and drug up. On a side note, I would never let my children (if I had any) listen to his music. It's just downright inappropriate.

A famous black movie director out in Los Angeles, whom I met during the Vibe Awards in 2005 when I was nominated for Vibe Vixen of the Year, called me after I gave him my card. He seemed thrilled to meet me. When I returned to the East Coast, he had told me to call him.

When I returned home, the director I met at the Vibe Awards and I started corresponding. Initially, we went back and forth through e-mails, then we started talking on the phone. I didn't have but maybe three phone conversations with him. After the first conversation, I knew he wasn't willing to help me with my career unless we could hang first.

"I'm a big fan of yours. So do you live in Atlanta?" he asked.

"No, I live in South Carolina."

"What part?"

"Spartanburg."

"Oh, I have family there. How often are you there?"

"Not much. I'm on the road a lot."

"I can fly over there to see you."

"That would be cool. I'll let you know when I'm home again. I would love to get into acting."

"I can help you with that when I come out to see you."

I wondered how in hell he could help me with acting in South Carolina. Ain't shit in South Carolina, and he knows it! He continued to talk about us hanging out and going to eat dinner. I wanted to tell him so badly that he was not getting any pussy and I'm not hungry and I don't need him to take me out to dinner!

I get so aggravated with these men and their one-track minds! After the first or second conversation, I knew that unless I was willing to meet him in the bedroom, there was no hope of working with him or getting a connection. This is one of the main reasons I don't go to industry parties or functions. If you're not trying to go home with someone that night, then you might as well forget them calling you about work. This is not true for every situation, but if you're an attractive female, forget it.

I'm very flattered that people find me attractive and fuckable, but at the end of the day, how is that helping me? I can't just be fucking these celebrities like a lot of models do. What's the purpose? If I want a dick that bad, then I can just call up one of my old flames and fuck them—at least I won't feel a certain way when I get up and go home the next morning.

If I fuck a celebrity or a million-dollar nigga, then I'm going to feel cheated and stupid the next morning, and here's why: If all I'm looking for is dick and a good fuck (which I rarely do), then why should I fuck some celebrity or athlete that doesn't give a fuck about me, never took the time to get to know me, isn't making my career or bank account any bigger, never has quality time for me, won't ever marry me, and I'm just another model or female he can add to his already-long list? Why? If I'm going to be fucking just for the hell of it, then I would rather fuck a nigga who knows and supports me.

I would rather fuck a nigga who appreciates my pussy than a nigga who just wants it because he's a celebrity and he thinks that he should have it. I wouldn't even enjoy sex if I know the nigga I'm with don't give a fuck about me whatsoever. I might as well go back to Club Nikki. I guarantee I'd end up with more money in my pockets than if I screwed around with an industry player for cash, cars, and condos.

I don't need to be linked to a celebrity that is not doing anything to build my future. Most of the models who settle for less every day wonder why they can't get anywhere. They think for some reason that fucking and sucking is the only way to go. Don't get me wrong; it all comes down to how I'm going to feel about myself at the end of the day. If you're going to sleep with a celebrity or you just feel like you have to because of their name and status, all I ask is that you sleep with one that can advance or help your career in some manner. A dick is a dick, and a stupid ho is a stupid ho, and that's what you're going to be in this industry if you're fucking these celebrities and not getting shit out of it!

Even the short period I dealt with Chad, Kayslay, or Gucci, they all helped me with my career in some form or fashion. If I'm going to deal with an industry nigga these days, then he has to help support where I'm trying to go in life. There is just too much headache trying to date most of these dudes in the industry to not get compensated in other ways besides just being in their company. Most of them don't want a real relationship anyway because they're married or already have live-in girlfriends that they're not trying to leave.

If I know a nigga has major money and power and he tells me he can't help me, then that's fine, I'll respect that to the fullest—but don't call me at three in the morning asking me if you can come to my hotel room. Don't ask to take me out to dinner. No, we can't hang out, and no, you can't fly me to your location. Go and find another model who just wants to be with you because you're a celebrity. I'm not pressed.

I personally know models that sleep around with these rappers and celebrities, and they don't even have a reliable car or can't even afford to pay their rent. I knew this one chick who told me she was fucking this very famous rapper, and he wouldn't even help get her AC unit fixed in her apartment. This was during the summer when the temperatures peaked at 100 degrees. She would brag to everyone that she was fucking him at every opportunity that she got. There's no dick in this world to make me sit in a hot-ass apartment, knowing that I'm fucking a nigga that's worth $30 million. I wonder how in hell she could fuck a nigga that's worth that much, but she had a $10-fan sitting in her window, trying to keep cool.

I look at it like this: if I have to be broke, homeless, and without transportation, than that's much easier for me to deal with than being broke, homeless, and without transportation—but I just fucked a dude who's a millionaire that told me he loves me. Ha! It's not going to happen! I can't understand these models. You're doing all this fucking just so you can say you fucked this rapper or that celebrity? I'm not perfect, but I'm not a fool, either. A broke dick feels just as good as a rich one to me, but at the end of the day, if I had some rich dick and didn't gain anything else, then I'm a little salty at myself. Having memories floating in your head of sleeping with some famous celebrity is probably all most of these females need, but remember, you can't take those memories to a car dealership or to your mortgage company, because they don't accept memories as a form of payment.

Yes, Karrine Steffans did it, but you're not her. You're you, so be a smart you. If you're going to be in this industry, work smart, not hard. I didn't dabble much with the celebrity side of the industry as far as sex went. I had my times, and I'm not bragging or saying what I did was right, but it is what it is. Nope, I didn't get a wedding ring (didn't want one) or notoriety (wasn't looking for it), but I did it, it was fun, and no, I don't regret it one bit.

People often ask me how I feel about Karrine Steffans and the impact she had on the industry. Do you want me to be honest, or do you want me to say what I think people want me to say? Well, I have a need to be real and tell how I feel about Karrine Steffans and her story since I've been asked a thousand times how I feel about it. In so many words, she wasn't known to any of us until she decided to go public with her accusations about the hip-hop community. Do I condone what she did? "No," but do I look at her in a negative way because she decided to tell on everyone? "No." These guys weren't kids that she was talking about in her book. They were all grown men; most of them were married and had girlfriends, and they should have known better. If you're out here sleeping around and get caught, then that's your fault, and that's the chance you have to take. You cheat, you get caught. You act like a dog, so Karrine shows the world how your bark compares to your bite.

Every woman knows how guys feel about sex. Some women think that if they give up sex, they can get far in this industry. It may work for some, but not most women. I can't say if I had slept with some of these dudes that my career would be better than it is now, because there is no real way of knowing. All I can say is be smart and follow your mind. Don't end up being a ho and at the end of the day, you're right where you started.

I get confused myself sometimes, because I don't know the answers to the question, "to sleep around or not to sleep around?" and I don't think anyone does. It's been proven to work, but it comes with its pros and cons. It's like gambling with your pussy. Sometimes you may win, sometimes you may lose. But at the end of the day, it's your decision. This world is crazy. Just ask yourself, is it worth fucking five guys to get to Beyoncé's or Halle Berry's status? I bet a good number of women would think "Absolutely."

In the beginning, Karrine wasn't famous. She wasn't a household name, and she certainly wasn't doing anything to help her establish the professional and financial independence that many women, inside and outside of this industry, work their asses off to get.

I'm not a fan of Karrine's, but I don't feel any particular way about her. She made those choices, and she lived that life. I don't think it affected me directly. America as a whole has never looked at video girls in a positive light. It's not Karrine's fault. It's all our faults, as a whole. The models, the rappers, the record labels, the groupies (can't leave them out), and the fans all feed the beast. Yes, I do agree that Karrine played her part in making it worse, especially by claiming she fell victim to the vicious Hollywood scene and then capitalizing off of her story, but the damage is done, and I don't even know how the image of a video girl will ever be repaired. Do we blame the rappers for their degrading lyrics? Maybe not. I think it goes back much further than that.

Maybe women in the industry need to handle their images and careers better. If you want respect, you have to demand it. Video girls audition for these music videos, knowing that the lyrics are degrading to females. But they don't care. They say, "Fuck it! I want to be on TV!" Then when they get on these video sets, they go wild because they can't control their hunger for stardom. They try to fit in and be accepted by other models, the production crew, and the artists, and end up being passed around. No, I don't blame the rappers entirely, because if we stop doing their videos, then they would stop with the degrading lyrics. You don't see the professional white models being degraded and called hoes and bitches, at least not the last time I checked. They don't have as deeply negative images as black video girls.

I don't have any Superhead stories of my own and probably never will, but I know models out here right now that are fucking, and after having fucked just as many men as Superhead, they will never have the money she has. No, it's not all about the money, but if you going to be a ho, be a paid ho. Have something to show for all the dicks you took besides a worn-out pussy and a piece of bubble gum.

I was able to somehow become an icon without all the sex, drugs, and bad rumors. My attitude has gotten me farther than I could have ever imagined, and it has made all the difference in keeping me above the Superhead nonsense.

# Chapter Twenty-One

I will never be able to count how many times a female has walked up to me and asked me how to build a body like mine. I get dozens of e-mails every single day from females asking me about my body, exercise, and nutrition.

"Buffie, I just had a baby. Can you help me get my stomach flat again?"

"Buffie, how do I lose weight without losing my ass?"

"Buffie, how can I get booty like yours?"

"Buffie, how can I gain weight?"

The questions are endless. I've never had the time to answer all these questions because I'm on the road like crazy and I'm never on my computer as much as I want to be. In the last year or so, I've been interacting with my female fans more. First of all, I *know* how it feels to be in a body that you don't love or you feel that you're not 100 percent pleased with. I was skinny and almost flat-chested, so I had the worst at both ends. Even my best friends used to wonder when I would ever get breasts. I use to beg my mother to buy me a bra just so I could wear one like my friends, knowing damn well I didn't have anything to put in it. I didn't have hips or ass, and you already know how I felt about that: HORRIBLE.

Guys would never push up on me like they would the fully developed girls, and I felt insecure as hell and flat-out ugly. The girls with the bodies seemed so happy with no worries, while I was always unhappy. I had a crush on a boy named Derrick in high school, and he used to tell me that I needed to eat. In other words, he was telling me I was skinny, which, in my world, *wasn't* a good thing. I remember him dating a girl name Felicia that was thick and had curves. I felt inadequate for years and years and people don't always have nice things to say when your body is not in shape.

In case you haven't guessed yet, I'm very passionate about the subject of gaining weight because gaining weight was one of the most rewarding things I have ever done as far as my body goes. I didn't have an overweight issue, I had an underweight issue, and it was just as bad as being overweight because people showed me no slack. If you're too fat, they laugh and say you're greedy and you need to stop eating. If you're skinny, people think you have an eating disorder or a strange medical condition or maybe you're doing drugs. I hated that shit!

Back when I was skinny and wanted so badly to gain weight, there wasn't much plastic surgery going on that I could remember. There wasn't such a thing as getting butt implants or injections. Shit, girls weren't even wearing hair weaves, at least not in Athens. Back then, you either had it or you didn't, but now if you don't have it, you can go and buy it. I wanted to gain weight because I hated the way I looked, but it seems like now, being thin is trendy. People get plastic surgery just to keep up with society. No one wants to hear the right way to gain or lose weight, they want the fastest way. Often, women are not changing for themselves, but for magazines, TV, music videos, or because someone else thinks they should change. That's crazy! Do it for yourself!

When I first started gaining weight, it came on all at once. I went from 119 lbs to 143 lbs quick, but I still wasn't satisfied. I continued to try to gain weight, and I did. I've been at 162 lbs for years. I've been as heavy as 174 lbs, but I had to lose weight because I felt fat. My ass was huge, but so was the rest of my body, including my stomach.

I've been exercising ever since I've gained weight. I stopped a few times, but was always forced to start back because my body would start getting out of shape. I would get love handles, my stomach would get big as hell, and my thighs were a mess. I even started wearing Spanx just to hold my stomach and make it look flat. The only problem with Spanx is if someone gave me a hug or put their arms around me to take a photo, then they could feel that I had it on, so I stopped wearing it. For all the females who don't know what Spanx is, it's a brand of compression pantyhose that helps shape your waist, stomach, and thighs. I have about two or three pair on deck just in case I get lazy again.

I'm from the South, and it isn't cute to be skinny in the South. I work very hard to maintain the weight that I have now. People who are obese know how hard it is to lose weight. Well, I'm speaking for everyone who is thin or underweight when I say that it's just as hard, or even harder, to gain weight.

We all know that calories are what help you gain weight. You have to have enough of them, and the people who can't gain weight are probably not consuming enough. I can't tell you how many calories to consume to gain weight because every body is different, but I can say make sure they're healthy calories. Even though junk food will help you gain the weight you want, you don't want to be unhealthy or develop some illness from unhealthy eating habits. I drink Boost daily, which is a nutrition drink with 360 calories a pop. It comes in different flavors, but I like chocolate. Boost is known to help maintain your weight, so that's why I drink it. I haven't had any health issues as of yet, and I thank God every day for that.

My favorite foods are everything that's bad for you. I

love soul food: fried chicken, pork chops, mac and cheese, and rice and gravy. I don't eat as much of that anymore, but I haven't given it up completely. I just watch how much of it that I eat. I eat a lot of baked meats instead of frying. I do eat healthier than I used to, but I know I still have improvements to make as I get older.

Exercising is not as hard to do as eating right is. I will get my ass up and hit the gym with no problem two to three times a week. I always do cardio to warm up before I start my resistance training. I personally do not do cardio every day, but some people do. Cardio helps me burn fat and burning fat makes you lose weight. I only do cardio three to four times a week when I'm trying to lose fat. If you have fat on your stomach, then you'll probably need to lose some weight. You will never ever see a toned flat stomach until you lose fat in that area. Even if you're doing crunches every single day, you will never see the results until you lose the fat that lies on top of the muscles in your stomach.

I work my entire body, but my main focus is on my hamstrings (the backs of my thighs), my quadriceps (the fronts of my thighs), my midsection, and my glutes (my butt). I don't work these muscles every day because it's just as important to let these muscles rest and repair as it is to work them. I usually do three or four sets of each exercise and between eight and twenty reps of each. As far as how many pounds you need to work with, this will vary from person to person. It all depends on what you're comfortable with without hurting yourself. My advice would be to talk to a professional trainer and he/she can instruct you on your ideal weight size. I do squats, leg presses, deadlifts, crunches, the plank, side crunches, bicycles, and kickbacks. I have a Web site, *www.buffiesbodyshop.com*, where I have video clips and tips on most of these exercises.

My butt hasn't always been this round and firm. It comes from exercising and building my muscles over the years. I have a trainer in D.C., Georgia, Indiana, and South Carolina. I still meet with each of them on a regular basis.

If anyone tells you that you can't build a bigger butt, they're telling you a lie. I know for a fact you can make the muscles in your butt bigger than what they are just like you can any part of your body that has muscles. Squats are one of the most basic exercises for the butt, but there are also different variations to the squat. Like I said earlier, the proper form to do any exercise is very, very important for efficiency and to keep you from risking injury.

Women look to me for guidance on exercising, and I'm going to tell them everything I've learned over the years in my new workout DVD, Bootynomics 101. My trainers have been very patient and focused with me over the years. They taught me everything I know about building and sculpting my body, and I'm finally in the position where I can share it with other females.

Women that e-mail me don't want to be skinny like women in most fitness tapes. I know I wouldn't buy a DVD with some skinny chick on the cover if I were trying to get a bigger and shapelier butt. Mel B's video will only be great for women who want to look like her. Why would I listen to a woman with a flat ass if I wanted a bigger butt? I would most likely listen to a woman who has a big booty than a woman who doesn't. I'm going to listen to a woman who isn't working out to be thin, but working out to get and stay shapely in a healthy way. The year 2009 is for women to truly embrace their shapely curves, and I'm supporting all the fine asses out there. Stay proud, ladies!

# Chapter Twenty-Two

So, there you are. The Vixen Icon has shared her soul. And now, after reflecting on my past, it's time to look to the future.

Having a stable, concrete, happy, and healthy foundation is my goal. No, I didn't go to school and get it the traditional way, but that was my choice, and I've appreciated shit a lot more when I look back and really grasp just what and how I did this. I've travelled the "not so traditional" roads in life just to be, at the end of the day, as successful as any other woman trying to get it out here.

I can't be a model forever. I don't want to be pigeonholed like a great number of urban models. There is nothing holding us back from doing other things besides putting on a bathing suit, posing for a magazine, or dancing in a music video. We do have options, and we do have minds, and we need to start employing them.

Being a dancer and traveling on the road so much has taught me how to handle people, and it made me strong in the streets. It gave me a lot of street knowledge and common sense that you can't learn in school. If I hadn't been dancing, I wouldn't be modeling because I wouldn't have met the people who made this happen for me. I don't know what in the world I'd be doing now if I weren't modeling. I don't know if I could ever work in a supermarket or in an office for forty hours a week again. I've been free too long, and I just can't go back to punching a clock. I would die if I had to go back to a regular job. I have to be able to move around and be free to make moves when I need to. A full-time job would just hold me back. And after helping elect Barak Obama, I feel like there isn't anything on this earth I can't do. I don't see limitations anymore!

I will never regret anything I've ever done in my life. I believe everything happens for a reason. I may not always know the reason, but it doesn't matter. I've made mistakes like hell in my life, but I promise you one thing: I did learn from my mistakes, and my mistakes made me a better person. I don't have a perfect life, but I'm happy and I love God and I know He has my back no matter what.

My life has changed so much in the last 5 years. I actually have a bright future to look forward to. I feel like I had to go through the things I went through to have the positive mind-set I have today. My self-esteem is much higher, my health is good, my family is supportive, and I'm financially stable. I'm by no means rich. Matter of fact, I still consider myself at the bottom when it comes to what I'm worth. That's why I continue to work hard and stay determined, because after seeing a black president in the Oval Office, I have in me more drive than ever to not stop working hard and achieving my goals.

From time to time, I may go in a strip club and hang out with my homies. When I'm there, sometimes I just sit, watch, and reminisce on old times. I think how lucky and fortunate I am that I overcame that lifestyle and I'm doing greater things. I still respect that hustle because I know the ones who really don't belong there are miserable as hell. I know I was miserable my last few years of dancing. I got tired of asking niggas for money. I got tired of guys touching me when I didn't want to be touched. I've had men kiss and even lick my ass when I turned my back to them, and they would often reach their hands below my waist when I sat on their laps. I got tired of being fake and smiling at niggas and telling them what they wanted to hear just to get in their pockets. I got tired of the unsanitary dressing rooms and clubs. I got tired of having to be so close to hating-ass females every night, knowing that they despised me and my body. I hated how my feet used to ache terribly after dancing in heels for hours on end, and how I could barely walk to my car after the club, let alone try to press on the gas and brake pedals.

Right now, if I pick up a magazine and pointed out ten urban models' interviews, I bet you the majority of them will say they are trying to be an actress. There's nothing wrong with that; by all means, follow your dreams to the end, but don't let that be the only thing you try to do, and don't think that's the only thing you can do. I can tell you now it won't be easy trying to be the next Halle Berry, so please know that. I've said in some of my interviews in the past that I wanted to be an actress; however, after I saw and realized I would not only have to make huge changes to my image, but also I still wasn't guaranteed stardom, so I wasn't ready to take the risk. I've never considered myself fat, and I didn't know if I was ready for a bunch of white people and directors in Hollywood telling me to lose weight because me and my ass are too fat.

Keep in mind that if for some reason your plans don't work out the way you wanted, always have plan B and C ready to execute. One of my future goals is to own a franchise of sport bars, sort of like Hooters but a little more urban. Instead of the slim white girls dominating, I would like a mixture of females from all nationalities. I would love to go for thicker, shapelier females and let people know that it's okay to have meat on your bones.

I also want to teach women how to stay in shape in

their forties and beyond. I've been doing a pretty good job at keeping my weight down and keeping my butt looking good. If I know anything in this world, women (especially black women!) want a nice round ass. Even white women want them now. I work on my stomach and my ass more than anything else on my body. I could easily teach and tell women how I do it and how they can do it.

We as urban models don't have the same avenues and opportunities as white models or glamour models. This means we have to work extra hard to get not even half of what they can get. I still say being black in America is much harder than being white, and my thoughts will never change about that. That's why I've never compared or measured myself or my success to models that are not black because it's not an even comparison. I feel that white models will always have a better chance at getting mainstream opportunities than black models. I won't let that stop me and deter me from what I want in life; it just makes me work harder.

I can't compare myself to a runway model because I'm not anything close to one. But even those models had to stop depending on their looks and start using their minds and diversifying. When I lie in the bed at night, I sometimes flip through the TV channels and see some of those formal runway models doing their thing. Cindy Crawford has her own line of furniture, workout tapes, and a skincare line. Tyra Banks has her own talk show, production company, and reality show. Heidi Klum designed her own fragrance, designed her own clothing line with Jordache, and is an author. Iman has her own cosmetic line, handbag line, and also a clothing line.

I used to be foolish with my money. I was so careless when it came to how I budgeted and saved. My credit was horrible, and I was broke, regardless of how much cash I had when I left the strip club. As soon as I made money, I would spend it because I knew that all I had to do was go right to the club that night and make it again. In my mind, money was so easy to make, so why did I have to save it?

I checked my credit scores a couple of months ago, and I had an average score of 810. I just smiled to myself. I was so proud! I started a Roth IRA a few years back, and I even have a financial advisor. I bought my first home in 2006. It's not the ultimate dream house, but I know it's coming because I'm always striving for better things in life.
I've started to think of other things that I enjoy doing that could help empower, enlighten, and make us ladies feel good about ourselves. I have to show women that we can't depend on our looks and our bodies, only our minds and intelligence.

I could be somewhere still stripping in a club, but I'm not. I know so many girls that came into the modeling game the same time I did, and they didn't make it. They tried, but nothing happened. Maybe they didn't have enough drive, or maybe they did something wrong. I know hundreds of them. Like I said, this game isn't for everyone, and the majority of budding models aren't going to shine and excel in the industry. Just like I'm not going to shine and excel in everything I try out.

It was meant for me to do this. You can't stop destiny and you can't stop something that's just meant for you; it'll move on with or without you. If you don't hop on board you'll miss the opportunity to change your life and increase your circle of influence. I jumped in and took it for what it was worth. I appreciate my blessing, and I thank God every day.

Whatever path a person chooses to get to the top is fine just as long as they get there with dignity. I tell people "Whatever you are, be the best at it." I want to be known as the stripper-turned-model that made it in this world. The female who did what no one thought was possible coming from her background. I want all women, from the prostitutes to business executives, to be able to relate to me in some form or fashion. Here it is, almost 5 years after my photos leaked onto the Web, and I've never stopped running. Ladies stay true to yourselves, and if you're doing what you know to succeed in life, then never, ever have any shame in your game.

# ORDER FORM
*Triple Crown Publications*
PO Box 247378
Columbus, OH 43224
1-800-Book-Log

| NAME | |
|---|---|
| ADDRESS | |
| CITY | |
| STATE | |
| ZIP | |

| | TITLES | PRICE |
|---|---|---|
| | A Hood Legend | $15.00 |
| | A Hustler's Son | $15.00 |
| | A Hustler's Wife | $15.00 |
| | A Project Chick | $15.00 |
| | Always A Queen | $15.00 |
| | Amongst Thieves | $15.00 |
| | Betrayed | $15.00 |
| | Bitch | $15.00 |
| | Bitch Reloaded | $15.00 |
| | Black | $15.00 |
| | Black and Ugly | $15.00 |
| | Blinded | $15.00 |
| | Buffie the Body 2009 Calendar | $20.00 |
| | Cash Money | $15.00 |
| | Chances | $15.00 |
| | Chyna Black | $15.00 |
| | Contagious | $15.00 |
| | Crack Head | $15.00 |
| | Cream | $15.00 |

**SHIPPING/HANDLING**
**1-3 books $5.00**
**4-9 books $9.00**
**$1.95 for each add'l book**

**TOTAL        $_____**

**FORMS OF ACCEPTED PAYMENTS:**
**Postage Stamps, Personal or Institutional Checks &
Money Orders.**
**All mail-in orders take 5-7 business days to be delivered.**

## ORDER FORM
*Triple Crown Publications*
PO Box 247378
Columbus, OH 43224
1-800-Book-Log

| | |
|---|---|
| NAME | |
| ADDRESS | |
| CITY | |
| STATE | |
| ZIP | |

| TITLES | PRICE |
|---|---|
| Cut Throat | $15.00 |
| Dangerous | $15.00 |
| Dime Piece | $15.00 |
| Dirty Red **Hardcover** | $20.00 |
| Dirty Red **Paperback** | $15.00 |
| Dirty South | $15.00 |
| Diva | $15.00 |
| Dollar Bill | $15.00 |
| Down Chick | $15.00 |
| Flipside of The Game | $15.00 |
| For the Strength of You | $15.00 |
| Game Over | $15.00 |
| Gangsta | $15.00 |
| Grimey | $15.00 |
| Grindin' **Hardcover** | $10.00 |
| Hold U Down | $15.00 |
| Hoodwinked | $15.00 |
| How to Succeed in the Publishing Game | $20.00 |
| In Cahootz | $15.00 |
| Keisha | $15.00 |

**SHIPPING/HANDLING**
**1-3 books $5.00**
**4-9 books $9.00**
**$1.95 for each add'l book**

TOTAL          $_____

**FORMS OF ACCEPTED PAYMENTS:**
**Postage Stamps, Personal or Institutional Checks & Money Orders.**
**All mail-in orders take 5-7 business days to be delivered.**

# ORDER FORM

*Triple Crown Publications*
PO Box 247378
Columbus, OH 43224
1-800-Book-Log

| NAME | |
|---|---|
| ADDRESS | |
| CITY | |
| STATE | |
| ZIP | |

| | TITLES | PRICE |
|---|---|---|
| | Larceny | $15.00 |
| | Let That Be the Reason | $15.00 |
| | Life | $15.00 |
| | Life's A Bitch | $15.00 |
| | Love & Loyalty | $15.00 |
| | Me & My Boyfriend | $15.00 |
| | Menage's Way | $15.00 |
| | Mina's Joint | $15.00 |
| | Mistress of the Game | $15.00 |
| | Queen | $15.00 |
| | Rage Times Fury | $15.00 |
| | Road Dawgz | $15.00 |
| | Sheisty | $15.00 |
| | Stacy | $15.00 |
| | Still Dirty ***Hardcover** | $20.00 |
| | Still Sheisty | $15.00 |
| | Street Love | $15.00 |
| | Sunshine & Rain | $15.00 |
| | The Bitch is Back | $15.00 |

**SHIPPING/HANDLING**
**1-3 books $5.00**
**4-9 books $9.00**
**$1.95 for each add'l book**

**TOTAL          $_____**

**FORMS OF ACCEPTED PAYMENTS:**
**Postage Stamps, Personal or Institutional Checks &**
**Money Orders.**
**All mail-in orders take 5-7 business days to be delivered.**

**ORDER FORM**
*Triple Crown Publications*
PO Box 247378
Columbus, OH 43224
1-800-Book-Log

| | |
|---|---|
| NAME | |
| ADDRESS | |
| CITY | |
| STATE | |
| ZIP | |

| TITLES | PRICE |
|---|---|
| The Game | $15.00 |
| The Hood Rats | $15.00 |
| The Pink Palace | $15.00 |
| The Set Up | $15.00 |
| Torn | $15.00 |
| Whore | $15.00 |
| | |
| | |
| | |
| | |
| | |
| | |
| | |
| | |
| | |
| | |
| | |
| | |
| | |

**SHIPPING/HANDLING**
**1-3 books $5.00**
**4-9 books $9.00**
**$1.95 for each add'l book**

**TOTAL        $_____**

**FORMS OF ACCEPTED PAYMENTS:**
**Postage Stamps, Institutional Checks & Money**
**Orders,  All mail in orders take 5-7 Business**
**days to be delivered**